coo big game

Scott & Tiffany Haugen

H E

*W*e would like to dedicate this book to the many cooks who have influenced our lives: our families, friends and the casual acquaintances we have made through work and travel. Most of all we would like to thank Tiffany's mom for trusting her in the kitchen at such a young age and Scott's mom for helping us clean up after our marathon test-kitchen cooking sessions. *May God bless you all!*

Spiral bound ISBN-13: 978-1-57188-407-7
Spiral bound UPC: 0-81127-00241-2
Book Design: Esther Poleo Design
Photography: Scott Haugen and Tiffany Haugen
Supplemental photos provided by John Hinderman
Back cover: John Hinderman
Printed in China

Originally Published by
Frank Amato Publications, 2007
Reprinted in 2015 by
Haugen Enterprises
P.O. Box 275
Walterville, OR 97489
www.scotthaugen.com
www.tiffanyhaugen.com

CONTENTS

INTRODUCTION

*T*he purpose of this book is to encourage cooks to expand their repertoire and discover the tasty pleasures of wild game. The dietary benefits of eating wild game are unmatched, be it due to their lean nature, lack of hormone-injected flesh or the fact that they are grown organically, free-range. Take a fine product such as wild game, and an open-mind in terms of how to properly prepare it, and the culinary delights which unveil themselves are limitless.

For many people, dealing with wild game brings with it the responsibility of handling meat solely on their own, from field dressing to processing to the final stages of preservation. When processing wild game, it's comforting to know only a few sets of hands have touched the meat. For a large number of folks, us included, even though we live in a modern, civilized society, there comes a certain level of satisfaction attained from living off wild game.

For generations our families have depended upon wild game as a staple in their diet. But since our marriage in 1990, the use of wild game in the Haugen household has continued to reach new levels. Two days after our honeymoon, we found ourselves living in one of Alaska's most remote villages, the Inupiat Eskimo settlement of Point Lay. We later moved to the village of Anaktuvuk Pass, serving as school teachers in these arctic settings.

In both villages we lived a subsistence lifestyle. On our way into the villages in August, we'd stop in Anchorage or Fairbanks and do all of our nine months worth of grocery shopping at once. As for meat, what we hunted is what we ate.

In Alaska our diet consisted of fish, waterfowl and ptarmigan, as well as occasionally gifted portions of whale, walrus and other Native-harvested game. But for the most part, it was the meat we hunted and processed on our own that got us through several years without a grocery store. Caribou, Dall sheep or moose constituted a daily source of protein in our diet, and when eating so much game meat, variety in the way it's prepared is the key to maintaining a love for what it has to offer.

During the summer months we'd travel the world on vacation. Often it was hunting that drew us to foreign countries, and while in these exotic locales, we took plenty of time to delve into the local culture and cuisine. It was during these journeys that we began studying the art of local cooking techniques and commonly used ingredients, especially how it was applied to wild game.

After Alaska, we thawed out by relocating to the island of Sumatra, Indonesia, where we spent four years

teaching at an international school. Though hunting was limited, we did manage to take our share of wild boar, and in fact, much preferred it over the imported beef supplies from nearby countries.

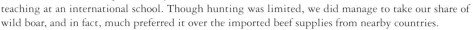

About the time we put our teaching careers on hold, in 2001, opportunities further opened up in the world of outdoor writing and television. Currently we travel to many states, Canadian provinces and other countries each year in pursuit of big game, and our desire to continually add to and perfect wild-game recipes never wanes. For our family, nearly all the meat we eat is what we hunt or fish for.

Combine all we've experienced and had to work with over the years, and the result is a compilation of more than 100 fine-tuned recipes. What makes this book even more special is the fact it is designed specifically for cooking wild game; the compilation of recipes are not simply tailored versions from cooking domestic meat. Translating these recipes into friendly terminology and easy-to-follow instructions means anyone can master them. In the end, we hope this book lends itself to encourage cooks to try new recipes and open up minds to how truly rewarding and delectable cooking with wild game can be.

*V*enison is the most commonly cooked big-game meat in North America, and in this section, the recipes are universal. From crop-fed whitetails to desert muleys, rutting blacktails, elk, caribou, moose, sheep, goats, bison, muskox and more, you'll find these recipes not only apply to a wide-range of species, but to animals of various ages. Remember, the final product is only as good as what you start with, and proper field care, combined with these recipes will result in some of the best-eating venison you have ever experienced.

VENISON

STEAKS WITH CAPER SHALLOT GRAVY

We were a bit hesitant when cooking a buck pronghorn taken in the rut, as we had heard mixed reviews on the meat. This recipe, developed specifically for the taste of antelope, combines a very flavorful marinade and gravy, and comes out delicious every time, regardless of the wild game used.

INGREDIENTS
- 1 pound venison steaks
- 1 cup Italian dressing (not fat-free)
- 2 tablespoons peanut oil

Place venison steaks in a sealable plastic bag with Italian dressing. Marinate 30 minutes to overnight (refrigerate if marinating over 30 minutes.) Prior to cooking let marinated venison sit at room temperature 30 minutes.

Gravy:
- 2 tablespoons butter
- 1/2 cup onion, diced
- 4 shallots, finely sliced
- 1/4 cup capers, chopped
- 2 tablespoons flour
- 1 cup beef broth
- 1 cup water
- 1/4 cup fresh parsley, chopped
- 1/2 teaspoon white pepper
- Salt to taste

In a large skillet, heat peanut oil on medium-high heat. Cook steaks to desired doneness, remove from pan. Prepare gravy in the same pan.

Gravy Preparation:
In heated skillet, melt butter on medium heat. Add onions and shallots and sauté until tender. Add capers and sprinkle flour evenly over skillet. Once mixture begins to bubble, slowly add beef broth and water, whisking constantly to prevent lumps from forming. Cook to desired consistency adding more liquid if needed. Remove from heat, add parsley, pepper and salt to taste. Pour gravy over cooked steaks or return steaks to pan and serve accordingly.

CANDY MEAT

The most memorable meal in the Fountain house was "candy meat." It was always served in celebratory fashion because any time a deer was shot in my family, it was shared by my dad, his two brothers and his father. We all celebrated the hunt by receiving a portion of the backstrap. It was also a memorable time because my father was always the one in the kitchen cooking dinner that night. He was the one who taught me how to make lump-free gravy as well as lump-free mashed potatoes. Lumps were a big no-no in the family and everyone strived to have gravy and mashed potatoes as smooth as Grandma Fountain's. Combine that with tender backstrap, and the meat tastes as good as candy.

Slice venison across the grain 1/4"-1/2" thick. Salt and pepper meat to taste. Dredge seasoned slices through flour, coating all sides. This can all be done at once just take care that the flour stays dry on the outside of the meat. Sprinkle more flour on the meat if needed. Heat a heavy skillet on medium-high heat. Melt butter and add venison carefully to avoid spatter. By the time all of the pieces are in the pan it is time to turn them all over. The pan is hot and the thinly sliced meat cooks very quickly. Once cooked, remove meat and place on a warm plate. Repeat the steps as needed for the rest of the meat. More butter may need to be added to the pan.

Pan Gravy:
After the meat has cooked, do not clean the pan, the drippings and brown bits you scrape up are what flavor the gravy. Add additional butter and melt. Using a wire whisk, whisk flour into the pan. Reduce heat to medium and whisk until smooth and bubbly. Slowly add milk, stirring continuously. After each 1/2 cup or so of milk, let the gravy thicken to desired consistency. When it thickens, add a bit more milk. Add remaining ingredients and serve over warm candy meat.

INGREDIENTS
- 1-2 pounds venison backstrap, thinly sliced
- 1/2 cup flour
- 1/4 cup butter
- Salt and pepper to taste

Pan Gravy:
- 1/4 cup butter
- 2 tablespoons flour
- 2-3 cups milk
- 2 teaspoons Kitchen Bouquet or Worcestershire sauce
- Salt and pepper to taste

CUTLETS WITH MARINARA SAUCE

As if it were yesterday, I still remember my Italian friend, Gina, teaching me how to make her dad's famous chicken cutlets. We have since adapted this recipe to every meat available and there never seems to be a leftover in sight.

INGREDIENTS

- 1-2 pounds venison backstrap
- 1/3 cup lemon juice
- 2 eggs, well beaten
- 1 tablespoon cold water
- 1 cup Italian bread crumbs
- 1/3 cup parmesan cheese, finely grated
- Black pepper to taste
- 6 cloves garlic
- 3 tablespoons olive oil
- 1/2 pound fresh mozzarella, sliced

Marinara Sauce:

- 2 tablespoons olive oil
- 1/2 onion, finely chopped
- 3 cloves garlic, pureed
- 1 cup diced tomatoes
- 3 tablespoons tomato paste
- 1/3 cup red wine
- 1/2 teaspoon Italian seasoning
- 1/4 cup parsley, chopped
- 8-10 fresh basil leaves, chopped
- Salt and pepper to taste

Slice venison backstrap into 1/2" cutlets. Between two layers of waxed paper, pound cutlets to 1/4". Prepare three shallow dishes for the three-step process. In the first dish, squeeze lemon juice. In the second dish, beat the eggs with water. In the third dish place bread crumbs, parmesan cheese and black pepper. Place pounded venison cutlets in lemon juice. In a heavy skillet, heat olive oil on medium-high heat. Brown garlic cloves 1-2 minutes to flavor oil and then remove from pan. One at a time, take cutlets from lemon juice, coat with egg mixture, press into bread crumbs to completely coat and add to hot oil. Cutlets are thin so they only need to cook 2-3 minutes per side. Immediately after cooking, top cutlet with mozzarella cheese, place under a hot broiler a few seconds if desired. Top or serve with marinara sauce on the side.

Marinara Sauce Preparation:

In a heavy skillet, heat olive oil on medium high heat. Sauté onion and garlic 2-3 minutes. Add remaining ingredients except for fresh basil. Bring sauce to a boil and reduce heat to low. Salt and pepper to taste. Simmer at least 15 minutes. Add basil during the last few minutes of cooking time.

CHICKEN-FRIED VENISON

Panko or Japanese bread crumbs can be a cook's best friend when cooking for children. In our experience, anything coated in panko using the following process will be eaten by children. From bear to bison, if it is fried using this recipe, there isn't a morsel left on the plate. Maybe we should try Brussels sprouts next. For a healthier fry, substitute canola oil for shortening.

Slice venison across the grain into 3/4" steaks. Between two layers of waxed paper, pound steaks to 1/2". Prepare three shallow dishes for the three-step process. In the first dish mix flour, seasoning salt and garlic powder. In the second dish, beat the eggs with the sour cream. In the third dish, place Japanese bread crumbs. In a large skillet, heat shortening on medium-high heat. One at a time, take venison steaks through flour mixture, then egg mixture and finally coat thoroughly with panko bread crumbs and add to hot oil. Steaks are thin and only need to cook 2-3 minutes per side. When steaks are done, use pan drippings to make country gravy.

Country Gravy Preparation:

Add additional butter to skillet and melt. Using a wire whisk, whisk flour into the pan. Reduce heat to medium and whisk until smooth and bubbly. Slowly add chicken broth, continuously stirring. When gravy begins to thicken, add milk continuously stirring. If a thick gravy is desired add less liquid, if a thin gravy is desired, add water. Season with salt and pepper and serve over steaks.

INGREDIENTS

- 1-2 pounds venison steaks
- 1/2 cup flour
- 2 teaspoons seasoning salt
- 1/2 teaspoon garlic powder
- 2 cups panko (Japanese bread crumbs)
- 2 eggs
- 1/3 cup sour cream
- 3 tablespoons shortening

Country Gravy:

- Pan drippings from Chicken Fried Venison
- 2 tablespoons butter
- 2 tablespoons flour
- 1 cup chicken broth
- 1 cup milk
- Salt and pepper to taste

GINGER COCONUT VENISON

Famed hunter, writer, TV host and game cook, Jim Zumbo shared that his favorite dish is ginger elk. Ginger is one of our favorite flavors with wild game. It complements a tender cut and reduces strong flavors in an older cut. The addition of coconut milk makes this dish rich and decadent.

INGREDIENTS

- 1-2 pounds venison steaks
- 1 onion, diced
- 2/3 cup ginger, minced
- 4 cloves garlic, minced
- 1/3 cup soy sauce
- 1 tablespoon sesame oil
- 1/2 cup flour
- 1/4 cup peanut oil
- 1 14-ounce can coconut milk

In a sealable plastic bag add steaks, onion, ginger, garlic, soy sauce and sesame oil. Marinate 2-8 hours. Using a fork, remove steaks one at a time from marinade mixture. Dredge in flour, keeping bits of onion and ginger on the meat. In a heavy skillet or Dutch oven, heat peanut oil on medium-high heat. Add floured venison and brown 5-7 minutes. Sprinkle in remaining flour and continue browning, until flour is mixed in. Turn heat to low, add coconut milk and simmer 30-45 minutes or until meat is tender. Serve over rice or noodles. Crock pot version: After browning meat and flour, place in a crock pot and add coconut milk. Cook on low heat 2-3 hours or until meat is tender, add water to thin if necessary.

PHILLY CHEESE STEAK PIZZA

An amazing combination of East Coast flavors, this pizza is like a trip down Philadelphia's famed South Street, from where we got the idea. Serve with marinara sauce on the side for a traditional version.

Slice venison thinly across the grain and into small strips. Spread venison out on a plate. Sprinkle liberally with steak or grill seasoning and drizzle olive oil on top. Mix the meat around to be sure all sides are coated with the seasonings and the oil. Set aside to marinate up to 30 minutes. Heat a heavy skillet on medium-high heat. Add all the venison and olive oil mixture at once. Sauté 1 minute and remove venison, set aside. Add onions, mushrooms and green pepper, sauté 1-2 minutes and remove from heat. In a small bowl combine sour cream, mayonnaise and minced garlic. Spread sour cream mixture evenly over prepared pizza crust. Sprinkle cheeses over the sauce. Distribute venison and vegetable mixture over cheese layer. Bake at 400° 16-20 minutes or until crust is lightly browned on the edges.

INGREDIENTS

- 1/2 - 1 pound venison, thinly sliced
- 3 tablespoons extra virgin olive oil
- Steak or grill seasoning
- 1/2 onion, thinly sliced
- 2/3 cup mushrooms, sliced
- 1/2 green pepper, thinly sliced
- 1/3 cup sour cream
- 1/4 cup mayonnaise
- 3 cloves garlic, minced
- 1 cup mozzarella cheese, grated
- 1/2 cup cheddar cheese, grated
- 1 prepared pizza crust

TRIPLE PEPPER STEAKS

This recipe can be made quickly as a stir fry if using a tender cut such as backstrap or tenderloin. But just in case that has been gobbled up, steaks cut from a roast will work as long as the meat is cooked until tender.

INGREDIENTS

- 1-2 pounds venison steaks
- 1 tablespoon olive oil
- 1 red pepper, chopped
- 1 green pepper, chopped
- 2 jalapeño peppers, diced
- 1 onion, chopped
- 2 tomatoes, chopped
- 1 can tomato sauce
- Dry mustard
- Salt & pepper
- Meat tenderizer (optional)

Liberally sprinkle steaks with dry mustard, salt, pepper and meat tenderizer (if desired). Let sit 20-30 minutes at room temperature. In a large skillet on medium-high heat, brown steaks in olive oil on both sides. Add remaining ingredients and reduce heat. Simmer, covered, 45 minutes to 1 hour. Serve over noodles, rice or sautéed polenta rounds.

RED CURRY WITH BASIL

When testing recipes for a cookbook, it's hard to avoid comparing and remain objective. Well, we both agree this one is very close to number one. It always takes us back to the memorable years we spent in Southeast Asia, dining on some of the world's most exquisite cuisine.

In a large skillet, heat peanut oil on medium heat. Add ginger and sauté one minute. Add red curry paste and brown sugar, sauté until bubbly. Add meat to curry mixture and brown. Reduce heat to low and add coconut milk. Simmer 45 minutes or until meat is tender. Remove from heat, add basil and serve over rice.

INGREDIENTS
- 1 pound venison, cubed
- 2 tablespoons peanut oil
- 1" fresh ginger, minced
- 1 tablespoon red curry paste
- 1 tablespoon brown sugar
- 1 can coconut milk
- 1/2 cup fresh basil, chopped

RED PEPPER MUSHROOM QUICK FRY

Thinly cut across the grain, even a tough piece of meat will turn out good if cooked for a short time. Tenderizer can be used prior to cooking in this recipe as well, just remember if using tenderizer, do not add salt.

INGREDIENTS

- 1 pound venison, cut into strips
- 1 red bell pepper, sliced
- 1 cup mushrooms, sliced
- 1/4 cup butter
- Seasoning salt to taste

Lightly season venison with your favorite seasoning salt. In a heavy skillet, melt butter on medium-high heat. Add venison, stir fry 1-2 minutes. Add mushrooms and peppers and stir fry an additional 1-2 minutes. Serve alone, over rice or over salad greens with vinaigrette dressing.

LEMON GRASS STIR-FRY

Cooking with lemon grass is certainly worth a trip to the Asian food market. However, fresh lemon grass and lemon grass in a tube is popping up at many local grocery stores. Lemon zest can be substituted but be aware, lemon grass adds a one-of-a-kind flavor that will leave you wanting more.

In a medium bowl mix all ingredients except chopped stalk of lemon grass. Marinate 6-12 hours. Prior to cooking let marinated venison sit at room temperature 30 minutes. Heat a skillet on medium-high heat. Add venison and all marinade. Stir fry until venison is browned on all sides. Add chopped lemon grass and stir fry an additional 2-3 minutes. Serve over rice or rice noodles. Remove chopped lemon grass before serving if desired.

INGREDIENTS

- I pound venison, cut in strips
- 2 tablespoons olive oil
- 2 tablespoons soy sauce
- 1 tablespoon rice vinegar
- 1 tablespoon lemon grass, minced
- 1 tablespoon ginger, minced
- 2 teaspoons brown sugar
- 1 stalk lemon grass, chopped

CERF AUX HERBS DE PROVENCE

Fellow hunter and author, Cork Graham, came up with this simple recipe that can be used for grilling, broiling or skillet frying venison. We found the flavors to work well with any venison and especially the gamey stuff. Cork adds a bit of liquid smoke if not cooking on the grill. He also uses this marinade for grilled vegetables.

INGREDIENTS

- 4-6 large venison steaks
- 1/2 cup Worcestershire sauce
- 1 tablespoon garlic powder
- 1 tablespoon onion powder
- 2 teaspoons Herbs de Provence
- 1 tablespoon sea salt
- Extra virgin olive oil

In a small bowl mix Worcestershire sauce, garlic powder, onion powder and herbs de Provence. Place venison steaks in a sealable plastic bag or container. Marinate overnight in refrigerator. Prior to cooking let marinated venison sit at room temperature 30 minutes. Remove steaks from marinade and sprinkle with sea salt. Coat with olive oil and place directly on a hot grill. Cook 2-3 minutes a side, turning only once. Recipe pictured here with sprouted-grain penne pasta in parmesan basil pesto sauce.

ITALIAN STEW

The second time we made this particular stew, we were filming a cooking segment for an outdoor TV show. We had just purchased new pans for the event and nearly had disastrous results when we discovered one pan was almost too small for the ingredients. All went well and once the stew cooked down, filled the pan just right. Once the show aired, we received emails from around the country, praising this recipe.

Dredge venison in flour, coating all sides, set aside. In a large stew pot, heat olive oil on medium-high heat. Add chopped onion and garlic. Sauté 2-3 minutes. Add floured venison and brown for 5-7 minutes. Add seasonings, stir gently. Slowly add beef broth, red wine, carrots and pearl onions. Bring mixture to a boil then reduce heat to medium-low. Add tomatoes and mushrooms. Simmer 2 hours on low heat until stew is thick and venison is tender. Serve with bread or over baked potatoes.

INGREDIENTS
- 2 pounds venison, cubed
- 1/2 cup flour
- 3-4 tablespoons olive oil
- 1 cup onion, chopped
- 4-6 cloves garlic, chopped
- 2 tablespoons Italian seasoning
- 2 teaspoons salt
- 1 tablespoon sugar
- 3 cups beef broth
- 2 cups red wine
- 1 cup pearl onions
- 1 cup carrots, sliced
- 1 can diced tomatoes
- 2 cups mushrooms, sliced

GRANDMA'S STEW

This recipe is a compilation of many of Grandma's recipes, one of which always uses the shortcut of prepared stew seasoning. Another uses leftover roast and makes a butter, flour and beef broth mixture as the thickener. When served with hot biscuits, this one is hard to beat.

INGREDIENTS

- 2 pounds venison, cubed
- 1/2 cup flour
- 1/4 cup peanut oil
- 2 tablespoons butter, optional
- 2 onions, chopped
- 2 cloves garlic, minced
- 4 carrots, peeled and chopped
- 4 potatoes, peeled and chopped
- 4 tablespoons Worcestershire sauce
- 2 teaspoons celery seed
- 5 bay leaves
- 4 cups water
- Salt and pepper to taste

Salt and pepper venison. Dredge venison cubes in flour, coating all sides, set aside. In a large stew pot, heat peanut oil on high heat. Add floured venison and brown for 5-7 minutes. Any extra flour can be added and browned at this time, add butter if desired. Add chopped onion and garlic. Lower heat to medium-high. Sauté 5 more minutes. Add remaining ingredients, cooking 5-10 minutes or until stew comes to a boil. Reduce heat to low and simmer at least 1 hour or place in a slow cooker for 3-5 hours. If stew gets too thick, thin with water or beef broth.

MEATY BLACK BEAN CHILI

Chili is one of those dishes in which our ingredients can vary, depending on what's in the pantry. This recipe, however, was tested and followed several times to perfection. When it comes to chili, this is a favorite.

In a heavy stew pot or Dutch oven, heat olive oil and sauté venison, onions and garlic on medium-high heat until meat is browned. Add spices, thoroughly combining. Add tomatoes and water and bring to a boil. Reduce heat to medium-low and simmer at least 30 minutes. Add black beans and simmer an additional 30 minutes. Garnish with sour cream, avocado or cheddar cheese, if desired.

INGREDIENTS

- 1 pound venison, ground or small cubes
- 2 tablespoons olive oil
- 1 onion, minced
- 3 cloves garlic, minced
- 3 tablespoons olive oil
- 1 tablespoon chili powder
- 2 teaspoons cumin
- 2 teaspoons unsweetened cocoa powder
- 1/2 teaspoon cayenne pepper
- 1/2 teaspoon coriander
- 1/2 teaspoon cinnamon
- Salt and pepper to taste
- 1 6-ounce can tomato paste
- 2 cups water
- 2 15-ounce cans black beans, drained

PANTRY BEANS

For many potluck entrees, we have come to rely on this quick, crowd-pleasing dish. Many times we have been asked for the recipe and it was one of those we always threw together with whatever was in the pantry, refrigerator and freezer. This version is a favorite. We have used all kinds of meat, including thuringer, beer sausage, ground venison, wild boar, wild turkey and ham chunks. The more variety of beans, the better. Try adding white beans, kidney beans, black-eyed peas or even lentils. Really, just use what's in the cupboard, it's hard to go wrong.

INGREDIENTS

- 1/2 pound bacon
- 2 cups onion, chopped or diced
- 1 pound venison, cubed
- 1 28-ounce can baked beans
- 1 15-ounce can pork and beans
- 1 15-ounce can pinto beans, drained
- 1 15-ounce can black beans, drained and rinsed
- 1 6-ounce can tomato paste
- 1 4-ounce can green chilies
- 1/4 cup cider vinegar
- 2 tablespoons spicy mustard
- 1 tablespoon molasses

In a large stew pot or Dutch oven, brown bacon on medium-high heat. Add venison and onions, cooking until venison is browned and onions translucent. At this point, all ingredients can be placed in a crock pot and cooked 2-5 hours on low heat. For the stovetop method, simply add remaining ingredients and bring to a boil. Reduce heat to low and simmer until venison is tender. Serve with cornbread.

OLD-FASHIONED POT PIE

"There is a bit of a yeasty flavor, I can't quite put my finger on it," commented more than one recipe taster. Beer drinker or not, the flavor that comes through in this pot pie is great. The Irish flair makes you feel like you are in a pub surrounded by lush green countryside.

Salt and pepper venison. Mix dry mustard with flour. Dredge venison in flour, coating all sides of the cubes, set aside. In a large stew pot, heat vegetable oil on high heat. Add floured venison and brown 5-7 minutes. Excess flour from dredging can be added and browned at this time. Add remaining ingredients, cooking 5-10 more minutes or until stew comes to a boil. Reduce to low heat and simmer 1 1/2 hours. Place filling mixture in a round casserole dish, top with pie crust and cut a few slits for steam to escape. Bake at 375° 30-40 minutes or until crust is golden brown.

INGREDIENTS

- 2 pounds venison, cubed
- 1/3 cup flour
- 2 teaspoons dry mustard
- 1/4 cup vegetable oil
- 1 onion, chopped
- 2 carrots, peeled and chopped
- 3 sticks celery, chopped
- 1 medium potato, peeled and cubed
- 1 small sweet potato, peeled and cubed
- 1 teaspoon fresh thyme or 1/2 teaspoon dried
- 3 bay leaves
- 1 14.5-ounce can diced tomatoes
- 2 cups dark ale or beef broth
- Salt and pepper to taste
- 1 10-inch prepared pie crust

SHEPHERD'S PIE

One-dish meals are a relief to the busy cook. If we can hit most of the four food groups and serve it all in one dish, it's a home run in our house. Pair this with some biscuits and a salad, and all bases are covered. Filling can also be made and served over mashed or baked potatoes.

The most efficient way to make this recipe is to prepare the mashed potatoes first or have them boiling while chopping and preparing the rest of the ingredients.

INGREDIENTS
Filling:
- 1 pound venison, ground or finely chopped
- 2 tablespoons olive oil
- 1/2 cup onion, chopped
- 2 cloves garlic, minced
- 1 cup mushrooms, chopped
- 1 cup peas
- 1/2 cup carrot, diced
- 1/2 cup celery, diced
- 1/2 cup bell pepper, diced
- 1/2 cup corn
- 2 tomatoes, chopped

In a medium skillet, heat olive oil on medium-high heat. Brown venison 2-3 minutes, add onion and garlic and sauté until tender. Add remaining ingredients and reduce heat to low. Prepare sauce and add to meat mixture.

Sauce:
- 2 tablespoons Dijon mustard
- 1 tablespoon Worcestershire sauce
- 1/2 cup beef broth
- 1/2 teaspoon salt
- 1/2 teaspoon lemon pepper
- 1 tablespoon cornstarch

In a small bowl, mix sauce ingredients until thoroughly combined.

Mashed Potatoes:
- 4 medium potatoes, peeled and quartered
- 2/3 cup sour cream
- 1/3 cup milk
- 1 cup cheddar cheese (reserve 1/3 cup for topping)
- Salt and white pepper to taste

In a large pot, boil potatoes in salted water until tender, about 15-25 minutes. Drain potatoes and mash, using a mixer, potato masher or ricer. Blend in sour cream and milk. Add cheese and stir gently. Salt and pepper to taste.

Spoon meat sauce mixture into a large, deep casserole dish. Top with mashed potatoes and reserved cheddar cheese. Bake at 325° 35-40 minutes.

VEGETABLE VENISON SOUP

After making a large venison roast, there are bound to be leftovers. Using cooked meat in soups cuts cooking time and adds moisture to the game. This simple soup is a healthy, low-fat, high-nutrient meal.

In a large pot, add broth and chopped vegetables. Bring to a boil and reduce to medium-low heat. Simmer 10-15 minutes or until veggies are almost tender. Add venison and simmer an additional 10-15 minutes.

INGREDIENTS

- 1 pound cooked cubed venison
- 2 medium potatoes, peeled and cubed
- 2 carrots, peeled and chopped
- 3 stalks celery, chopped
- 4 cups beef or vegetable broth
- Salt and pepper to taste

SPICY SPAGHETTI & MEATBALLS

Meatballs are fun. They are messy to make and quite labor intensive but they look great on the plate and instead of searching for the ground beef, it is obvious you get an entire serving of meat in 2-3 meatballs. Kids of all ages, adults included, rarely turn down meatballs.

INGREDIENTS

- 1 pound ground venison
- 1 egg
- 1 cup Italian bread crumbs
- 1/4 cup onion, minced
- 3 cloves garlic, minced
- 1 tablespoon olive oil
- 1 tablespoon Worcestershire sauce
- 1/2 teaspoon salt
- 1/2 tsp cayenne pepper
- 2 tablespoons olive oil for browning
- 8 ounces pasta, cooked

Sauce:

- 2 tablespoons olive oil
- 3 cloves garlic, chopped
- 1 teaspoon red pepper flakes
- 2 14.5-cans diced tomatoes with liquid
- 1 teaspoon fresh oregano
- 10-15 fresh basil leaves, chopped
- 2 tablespoons fresh parsley, chopped

In a large mixing bowl, thoroughly combine venison, egg, bread crumbs, onion, garlic, olive oil and spices. Shape into 15-20 meatballs. In a heavy skillet, heat 2 tablespoons olive oil on medium-high heat. Gently add meatballs, browning on all sides. Remove meatballs from skillet and set aside.

Add 2 more tablespoons olive oil to skillet. Sauté garlic and red pepper flakes on medium heat 3-5 minutes. Add diced tomatoes and oregano and bring to a low boil. Return meatballs to skillet. Reduce heat to low, cover and simmer 20-30 minutes. Add basil and parsley right before serving to maximize flavor. Serve over cooked spaghetti, linguine or angel hair pasta. Top with freshly grated parmesan cheese.

SWEDISH MEATBALLS

Grandma Bergstrom always makes Swedish meatballs for Christmas Eve. She challenges herself every year with trying new recipes for this particular dish. We used her expertise to come up with our own recipe, a combination of her many.

In a large mixing bowl, thoroughly combine venison, instant mashed potato flakes, egg, milk, onion, garlic and spices. Shape into 15-20 meatballs. In a heavy skillet, heat peanut oil on medium-high heat. Gently add meatballs, browning on all sides. Remove meatballs from skillet and set aside.

Stir soup mix into pan and mix with remaining oil. Add water and cook until bubbling. Return meatballs to skillet. Reduce heat to low, cover and simmer 20-30 more minutes. Serve over noodles, rice or as an appetizer, these keep warm in a crock pot on low heat.

INGREDIENTS

- 1 pound ground venison
- 1/3 cup instant mashed potato flakes
- 1 egg
- 1/3 cup milk
- 2 tablespoons onion, finely chopped
- 1 clove garlic, minced
- 1 teaspoon parsley flakes
- 1/2 teaspoon salt
- 1/4 teaspoon allspice
- 1/4 teaspoon nutmeg
- 1/4 teaspoon white pepper
- 3 tablespoons peanut oil
- 1 1-ounce package onion soup mix
- 1 1/2 cups cold water

HAM & SWISS BURGERS

It's nice to offer a change from traditional cheeseburgers. The surprise inside this meal adds flavor and complements the taste of wild game. Ground venison has many variations, add fat to pan if needed.

INGREDIENTS

- 1 pound ground venison
- 1 egg
- 2 tablespoons Worcestershire sauce
- 2 tablespoons red wine
- 1 teaspoon salt
- 1 teaspoon black pepper
- 4 slices Swiss cheese
- 12 slices Canadian bacon
- Thousand island dressing
- Lettuce, optional

In a medium bowl, combine venison, egg, Worcestershire, wine, salt and pepper. Form 8 thin patties. Place slice of Swiss cheese on top of patty and top with another patty taking care to seal, completely enclosing the cheese. In a large skillet or on a hot grill, cook burgers to desired doneness. Warm Canadian bacon and place atop burgers. Serve with Thousand Island dressing on a bun or use lettuce to make a wrap.

TOSTADA PATTIES

Never getting the hang of eating a tostada, we developed this recipe just for the purpose of keeping the meat on the tortilla! The recipe can be made into appetizers by using small, round tortilla chips and very small meat patties.

In a medium bowl, smash pinto beans with a fork. Add remaining ingredients and thoroughly combine. Make 4-6 patties for a tortilla shell or 10-15 patties for appetizers on a tortilla chip. In a large skillet or on a hot grill, cook burgers to desired doneness. Serve on sour-cream-topped tortilla with cheese, guacamole and salsa.

INGREDIENTS

- 1 pound ground venison
- 1 15-ounce can pinto beans, drained
- 2 cloves garlic, minced
- 1 egg
- 1 tablespoon chili powder
- 1 tablespoon cumin
- 1 teaspoon salt
- 10-20 shakes hot pepper sauce
- Oil for frying, if needed

Garnish:

- 1 cup cheese, grated
- 1 cup guacamole
- 1/2 cup sour cream
- 1/2 cup salsa

PIZZA HOAGIES

Reminiscent of a late-night stromboli delivery on the East Coast, these hoagies offer something deliciously different from a traditional pizza. Patties can be cooked ahead and reheated or kept warm in marinara sauce and served from a crock pot.

INGREDIENTS

- 1/2 pound ground venison
- 1/2 pound chorizo sausage
- 1/4 cup pepperoni, chopped
- 2 cloves garlic, minced
- 2 tablespoons tomato paste
- 2 teaspoons Italian seasoning

- Provolone cheese
- Hoagie rolls, toasted

In a medium bowl, combine all ingredients. Shape into 12-16 small patties (bigger than a meatball, smaller than a hamburger). In a large skillet or on a hot grill, cook patties to desired doneness. Place hot patties on a toasted hoagie roll and top with a slice of provolone cheese. Melt cheese under a broiler element if desired. Use pizza sauce or mayonnaise and ketchup as condiments.

BURGER DOGS

Shaped like a hot dog with completely identifiable ingredients? Yes, your kids and your guests will eat this. Try freezing these ahead of time for a quick meal on the grill. Seasonings can be adjusted to fit individual tastes.

If possible, grind all ingredients in a grinder using a medium plate. All ingredients can also be mixed in a large bowl by hand. Shape into hot dog size and grill or pan fry to desired doneness or an internal temperature of 160°. Serve on hot dog buns with all the traditional fixings.

INGREDIENTS

- 1 pound venison, ground
- 1/2 pound bacon, finely chopped
- 1 teaspoon red pepper flakes (optional)
- 1/2 teaspoon poultry seasoning
- 1/2 teaspoon black pepper
- 1/2 teaspoon salt
- 1/2 teaspoon coriander
- 1/2 teaspoon liquid smoke (optional)

Taking us back to a delicious elephant meat pie we had on our first trip to South Africa, this recipe makes a great portable meal and freezes well for a quick snack. For an easy recipe shortcut, substitute store-bought pizza or bread dough for the crust.

INGREDIENTS

Filling:

- 1 pound venison stew pieces
- 1/2 cup barbeque sauce
- 1 tablespoon spicy brown mustard
- 2 cloves garlic, chopped
- 2 tablespoons balsamic vinegar
- 1 teaspoon salt
- 1 onion
- 4 slices thick bacon
- 1/4 cup raisins
- 1 egg white, well beaten

Crust:

- 1 package active dry yeast
- 1 teaspoon sugar
- 1 1/4 cups warm water
- 3 1/3 cups white flour
- 1 1/2 teaspoons salt
- 2 teaspoons olive oil

In a medium bowl, mix barbeque sauce, mustard, garlic and vinegar. Add venison and marinate overnight. Using a food chopper, finely chop venison, leaving in marinade mixture. Add salt and onion, pulse until combined. Remove venison from food chopper. Chop bacon finely using the food chopper or a knife. In a skillet, on medium heat, cook bacon until slightly browned. Add venison mixture and fry until it is no longer pink. Remove from heat and gently stir in raisins. Cool slightly before stuffing crusts.

Crust Preparation:

In a small bowl, dissolve yeast and sugar in warm water. Let stand 5-10 minutes. In a large bowl mix flour and salt. Using a food processor or a mixer with a dough hook, combine the yeast mixture with the flour and salt. Mix until dough does not stick to the sides of the bowl. Make a ball with the dough and coat evenly with olive oil. Seal bowl with plastic wrap. Let dough rest 30 minutes to 1 hour.

Divide dough into 10-12 balls. Roll each ball into a 5-inch circle. Scoop 1-2 tablespoons of venison mixture onto each circle. Wet the exposed edges with egg white, fold over and crimp closed with a fork. Poke a few vent holes in the top of the meat pie and brush with egg white. Let pies sit and rise 10-20 more minutes. Bake at 425° 10-15 minutes or until golden brown. Serve with barbeque sauce for dipping.

CANNELLONI

Won ton wrappers make a great alternative to dried pasta that must be cooked prior to filling. Easy to assemble ahead and bake when needed this makes a great, quick, kid-friendly dinner. For a less sweet version, substitute tomato sauce for the condensed tomato soup.

In a medium skillet, heat olive oil on medium-high heat. Brown venison 2-3 minutes, add onion and garlic and sauté until tender. Add spinach, basil and Italian seasoning. Remove from heat and let mixture cool. In a medium bowl, combine sauce ingredients. Pour 1/3 cup of the sauce in the bottom of a casserole dish. For each cannelloni, spoon 1/4 cup meat mixture onto one end of a won ton wrapper, roll wrapper around filling. Place filled cannelloni, seam side down, into sauce in casserole dish. Once all cannelloni are filled, pour remaining sauce over top, completely covering any exposed won ton wrappers. Cover and bake at 350° 30 minutes. Sprinkle cheese on top during last 5 minutes of baking time.

INGREDIENTS

Filling:

- 1 pound venison, ground or finely chopped
- 1 tablespoon olive oil
- 1/3 cup onion, finely chopped
- 3 cloves garlic, minced
- 2 cups fresh spinach
- 1/3 cup fresh basil (optional)
- 1/4 teaspoon Italian seasoning
- 10 large square won ton wrappers
- 1 cup mozzarella or jack cheese, shredded

Sauce:

- 1 10 3/4-ounce can condensed tomato soup
- 1/4 cup white wine
- 1/2 cup beef broth
- 1/4 teaspoon Italian seasoning

PORCUPINE BALLS

More commonly known as "cabbage rolls," these were a regular dinner in Scott's home while growing up. Where the name originated, no one knows, but it continues in our house today. Hopefully there won't be too much disappointment when people realize that there is no actual porcupine meat in this recipe.

INGREDIENTS

Filling:
- 1 pound venison, ground or finely chopped
- 1 cup tomato sauce
- 1/2 cup instant brown or white rice, uncooked
- 1/3 cup onion, minced
- 2 cloves garlic, minced
- 1 7-ounce can sliced mushrooms, undrained
- 1 teaspoon sugar
- 1/2 teaspoon salt
- 1/4 teaspoon cinnamon
- 1/8 teaspoon allspice (optional)

Sauce:
- 1 cup tomato sauce
- 2 tablespoons water
- 1 tablespoon white vinegar
- 1 head cabbage or 10-12 large leaves

Prepare cabbage by soaking leaves in boiling water 5-10 minutes. Remove from water and let dry. In a small bowl, mix sauce ingredients. Pour 1/3 cup of the sauce into bottom of a casserole dish. In a medium bowl, mix all filling ingredients until thoroughly combined. For each porcupine ball, spoon 1/4-1/3 cup venison filling onto the edge of a cabbage leaf. Fold leaf over to completely enclose venison filling. Place, seam side down, into sauce in casserole dish. Once all leaves are filled, pour remaining sauce over top, completely covering cabbage rolls. Bake at 350° 45-50 minutes or until meat mixture reaches an internal temperature of 165°. Thicken pan juices for gravy, if desired.

LAYERED LASAGNA

Lasagna was the first meal I cooked for Scott when we were dating, he still can't decide if it was my lasagna or my chocolate chip cookies that sealed the deal. Sometimes we add a layer of zucchini or spinach to this recipe and omit 1/2 of the cheese to make it a lighter meal.

In a large skillet, heat olive oil on medium-high heat. Add ground venison and onions, cook until venison is browned and onions are soft. Add garlic and peppers, cooking 1-2 more minutes. Add remaining sauce ingredients and simmer 10-30 minutes. In a small bowl, or right in the carton, mix cottage cheese, egg, parsley and pepper. Grate cheeses into a bowl and gently mix. Cover the bottom of a 9" x 13" casserole baking dish with a thin layer of the meat/sauce mixture. 1) Layer 4 lasagna noodles across the pan, slightly overlapping. 2) Spread 1/2 of the cottage cheese layer evenly over the noodles. 3) Sprinkle 1/3 of the mixed-cheese mixture over the cottage cheese layer. 4) Spread 1/3 of the remaining meat sauce over cheese. Repeat steps 1-4. Add a final layer of noodles and top with the rest of the sauce. Be sure to cover all noodles with sauce so they don't get crispy while baking. Top with remaining cheese. Bake at 350° 35-45 minutes.

INGREDIENTS

Layer 1: Sauce

- 1 pound ground venison
- 3 tablespoons olive oil
- 1 onion, diced
- 3 cloves garlic, chopped
- 1/2 cup green peppers, diced
- 2 cans tomato sauce
- 1 jar sun-dried tomatoes, chopped or 1 6-ounce can tomato paste
- 2 teaspoons Italian seasoning
- 3-5 dashes of Tobacco sauce
- 1/2 cup water
- Salt and pepper to taste

Layer 2: Noodles

- 12 Wide Lasagna Noodles, cooked al dente
- Follow directions on package, cool slightly

Layer 3: Cottage Cheese

- 1 16-ounce container cottage cheese
- 1 egg, beaten
- 1 tablespoon dried parsley
- 1/2 teaspoon black pepper

Layer 4: Shredded Cheese

- 2 cups mozzarella cheese
- 1 cup cheddar cheese
- 1 cup parmesan cheese

PARMESAN-STUFFED BACKSTRAP

The key to this recipe is to not overcook the tender cut of meat. The plank will help by keeping in the moisture, but always use a meat thermometer. If you do not have enough backstrap to feed your crowd, this makes a nice hors d'oeuvre and is a great introduction to plank-cooked wild game.

INGREDIENTS

- 3-4-pound venison backstrap
- 3/4 cup caesar salad dressing
- 2 tablespoons onion, minced
- 2 tablespoons parsley, chopped
- 2 cloves garlic, minced
- 1 cup plain bread crumbs
- 3/4 cup parmesan cheese
- 2 teaspoons dry mustard
- 2 eggs, beaten
- 2 tablespoons white wine or water
- 1/2 teaspoon salt
- 1/4 teaspoon black pepper
- 1 cup spinach
- 1 prepared cooking plank, see page 118

Butterfly backstrap and pound between 2 pieces of waxed paper until 3/4 inch thick. Marinate in caesar salad dressing overnight. Prior to cooking, let marinated venison sit at room temperature 30 minutes. Mix all remaining ingredients except spinach. Remove backstrap from marinade and place on a prepared plank or ovenproof baking dish. Spread parmesan mixture evenly over backstrap. Lay spinach over the parmesan mixture and fold over at least one time. Coat venison with remaining caesar dressing. Grill or bake at 375° 20-25 minutes or until internal temperature reaches 165°. Let sit at least 5 minutes before slicing.

ROSEMARY-MARINATED KEBABS

When asked what to do with a gamey cut of venison, we always suggest strong herbs or spices. Rosemary is one of those flavor-packed herbs that we have paired with Dall sheep and wild goat with great success. If fortunate enough to have a sturdy, prolific rosemary bush, try using rosemary branches in place of skewers.

In a small bowl, mix red wine, mint, olive oil, garlic, vinegar, lemon juice, rosemary and black pepper. Place in a sealable plastic bag or airtight container with cubed venison. Marinate up to 12 hours. Prior to cooking let marinated venison sit at room temperature 30 minutes. Remove cubed venison from marinade. Thread skewers, alternating mushrooms, zucchini and cherry tomatoes as desired, leaving one inch on each end. Place skewers on prepared plank. Brush meat and vegetables lightly with oil. Grill or bake at 375° 10-15 minutes. Garnish with fresh mint and sprigs of rosemary, if desired.

INGREDIENTS

- 2 pounds venison, cubed
- 1/3 cup red wine
- 1/3 cup fresh mint, chopped
- 1/4 cup olive oil
- 8 cloves garlic, minced
- 2 tablespoons balsamic vinegar
- 2 tablespoons lemon juice
- 1 tablespoon fresh rosemary, finely chopped
- 1/2 teaspoon black pepper
- 10-15 whole mushrooms
- 2 small zucchini, chopped
- Cherry tomatoes (optional)
- Olive oil
- Metal or wooden skewers (soak wooden skewers overnight in water)
- 1 prepared cooking plank, see page 118
- Fresh mint and rosemary for garnish

PLANKED BLUE CHEESE TENDERLOIN

If you haven't tried venison on a plank, we urge you to do so. The flavor is the first thing you will notice and the moistness of the meat, a close second. After enjoying a meal, just throw the plank away for easy cleanup, unless it was used in the oven, in which case it can be reused.

INGREDIENTS

- 2-pound venison tenderloin
- 2 tablespoons red wine
- 4 cloves garlic, minced
- 1 tablespoon olive oil
- 1 teaspoon oregano
- Salt and pepper to taste
- 1/2 cup blue cheese, crumbled
- 1 prepared cooking plank, see page 118

Rinse meat and pat dry. Pierce venison tenderloin with a fork in several places. Place tenderloin in a sealable plastic bag. Add wine, garlic, oil and oregano. Seal bag and mix by hand. Marinate in refrigerator 3-12 hours. Prior to cooking, let marinated venison sit at room temperature 30 minutes. On a hot, well-greased grill, sear grill marks into tenderloin, about 1 minute per side. Place on a prepared plank. Grill or bake at 375° 15-20 minutes or until desired doneness, 145° (medium-rare) to 170° (well-done). Sprinkle crumbled blue cheese on top of tenderloin for last 5 minutes of cooking time. Let sit 10 minutes before slicing.

GARLIC-RUBBED ROAST

Not only is garlic one of the most commonly used flavors in the world, it has many health benefits.
We never pass up the opportunity to load our recipes with fresh garlic. If in a hurry, minced garlic
in the jar can be substituted, just be sure it's well drained.

Puree the rub ingredients in a food processor or mini-chopper. Pierce roast in many places with a fork. Coat roast completely with the rub mixture. Marinate in the refrigerator 6-8 hours. Prior to cooking, let marinated venison sit at room temperature 30 minutes. Place on a prepared plank, cover loosely with foil, tucking ends of foil 1/2" under plank to seal. Grill or bake at 350° 45 minutes to 1 hour or until desired doneness, 145° (medium-rare) to 170° (well-done). Let sit 10 minutes before slicing.

INGREDIENTS

- 1-1/2-pound venison roast
- 8-10 cloves garlic
- 1 tablespoon olive oil
- 1 tablespoon smoked paprika
- 1 tablespoon black pepper
- 1 tablespoon brown sugar
- 1 teaspoon salt
- 1 prepared cooking plank, see page 118

BACON DATE BITES

Always in search of appetizers that are easy to prepare and loved by guests—especially those who have not eaten a lot of wild game—we've found this recipe to serve both purposes. These are simple to prepare ahead of time and can be cooked right before guests arrive.

INGREDIENTS

- 1 pound venison, thinly sliced
- 1 pound bacon
- 20 dates
- 1/4 cup extra virgin olive oil
- 1/4 cup balsamic vinegar
- 1 prepared cooking plank, see page 118

Cut venison roast in long slices. In a small bowl or sealable plastic bag, mix extra virgin olive oil with balsamic vinegar. Add meat to oil and vinegar and marinate 6-12 hours. Prior to cooking, let marinated venison sit at room temperature 30 minutes. Cut bacon into half strips. If dates are large, they can be cut in half. Layer venison over bacon, place date on one end and roll. The bacon should be on the outside. Place on a prepared plank. Bake at 375° or grill until bacon is crisp, about 12-15 minutes. Bacon date bites can be broiled until bacon is crisp but do not use a plank if broiling.

STEW ON A STICK

We like many variations of the kebab. For camping we like to store frozen venison in the marinade so it not only stays cool and keeps, but is conveniently seasoned. Either cook this recipe on a plank or load up a stick and cook over an open campfire.

Place cubed venison in a medium bowl. Add gourmet sauce, tossing lightly. Let sit at room temperature 20-30 minutes. Steam or microwave potatoes and carrots until slightly soft, just enough to place easily onto the skewers. Thread skewers, alternating meat and vegetables, leaving one inch on each end. Place skewers on prepared plank. Brush meat and vegetables lightly with oil. Grill or bake at 375° 10-15 minutes. Serve with gravy on the side or poured over the meat and vegetable skewers.

INGREDIENTS
- 2 cups venison, cubed
- 1/4 cup Mr. Yoshida's Gourmet sauce
- 1 cup russet potatoes, peeled, cubed and precooked
- 1 cup carrots, chopped and precooked
- 1 cup celery, chopped
- 1/2 onion, chopped
- Olive or canola oil
- Metal or wooden skewers (soak wooden skewers overnight in water)
- 1 prepared cooking plank, see page 118

Brown Gravy:
- 3 tablespoons butter
- 3 tablespoons flour
- 1 1/2 cups beef broth
- 1 tablespoon Worcestershire sauce
- Salt and pepper to taste

Gravy Preparation:
In a medium skillet, melt butter on medium-high heat. Stir in flour and whisk until smooth. Lower heat to medium and slowly add beef broth. Cook 5 minutes at a low boil, continually whisking to avoid lumps. Stir in Worcestershire sauce, add salt and pepper to taste.

HOT SWISS PLANKED STEAK

Because the meat is protected by a plank and layer of vegetables, as well as another layer of vegetables on top, it retains it's moisture very well in this dish. Both the meat and vegetables in this recipe readily acquire smoke flavors, making for a delicious meal. We've enjoyed this with bison, bear and pronghorn meat, among others.

INGREDIENTS

- 4-6 1" venison steaks
- 1/2 cup red pepper, chopped
- 1/2 cup green pepper, chopped
- 1/2 cup onion, chopped
- 1 tomato, chopped
- 1-2 jalapeno peppers, chopped
- 2 teaspoons dry mustard
- 1/2 teaspoon salt or meat tenderizer
- Olive oil
- 1 prepared cooking plank, see page 118

Sprinkle dry mustard and salt, or meat tenderizer, over steaks and lightly pound with a meat mallet or tenderizing tool. Brush both sides of steaks with olive oil. In a small bowl, mix peppers, onion and tomato. On a hot grill or skillet, sear steaks 30 seconds on each side. Place half of pepper mixture on a prepared plank. Place steaks atop pepper mixture and top with remaining peppers. Grill or bake at 350° 20-25 minutes or until steaks reach desired doneness. Serve directly on plank if desired.

SAUERBRATEN

While much of the "pickling" of meats was traditionally done to preserve what could not be frozen or refrigerated, sauerbraten should not be overlooked for the unique and delicious flavor that it offers. Because of the heavy spices and pickling process, this recipe works well on any "gamey" cut of meat.

In a medium bowl, mix first eight marinade ingredients until sugar is dissolved. Place marinade and roast in a sealable plastic bag. Add vegetables and refrigerate 72 hours, turning at least two times a day. Remove roast from marinade, do not discard marinade. In a heavy skillet, heat oil on medium-high heat and sear roast on all sides. Strain marinade and add liquid to pot, discarding remaining vegetables and spices. Bring to a boil, reduce to medium-low heat. Cover and cook 2 1/2 hours or until venison is tender. Add cherries during the last 30 minutes of cooking time. Remove roast, let sit 10 minutes before slicing. Reduce or thicken pan drippings as needed for gravy.

INGREDIENTS

- 2-3-pound venison roast

Marinade/Cure:

- 1 cup red wine
- 1 cup red wine vinegar
- 1/3 cup soy sauce
- 2 tablespoons sugar
- 2 tablespoons pickling spice
- 1 teaspoon fresh ground black pepper
- 1 teaspoon salt
- 10 juniper berries, crushed (optional)
- 1 onion, sliced
- 2 carrots, sliced
- 2 stalks celery, sliced
- 2 tablespoons oil
- 1/2 cup dried cherries

O'MULLARKEY'S CORNED ROAST

Dear neighbors and friends, Larry and Elizabeth Mullarkey share this dinner with us every St. Patrick's Day. Once we corned the venison it was ready for all the final "Mullarkey touches." Though venison is suggested, this is one of our favorite ways to prepare bear roasts.

INGREDIENTS

- 4-6-pound venison roast, corned
- 4 cloves garlic, halved
- 1 teaspoon whole peppercorns
- 2 cups water
- 1 1/2 cups brown sugar
- 4 tablespoons brown mustard
- 4 tablespoons ketchup

Corned Venison:
- 4-6-pound venison roast
- 1/3 cup Morton Tender Quick
- 1/4 cup brown sugar
- 1 tablespoon pickling spices
- 1 tablespoon black pepper
- 2 teaspoons granulated garlic

In a small bowl, mix brown sugar, mustard and ketchup, set aside. Place the rinsed corned venison in a pressure cooker with water, garlic and peppercorns. Cook at 15 pounds pressure for 50 minutes, turn off heat and let the pressure go down on its own. (Alternative method: In a large pot, cover meat with water and cook on low heat 4-5 hours or until fork tender.) When venison is done, slice 1/2" thick and layer in a casserole dish. Cover venison completely with brown sugar mixture. Bake at 350° 25 minutes. Serve with fried potatoes, steamed cabbage and candied carrots.

Corned Venison:
Mix dry ingredients and rub into venison roast. Place in a sealable plastic bag. Refrigerate and allow to cure 5-7 days, turning bag over every day.

BRAISED VENISON

Flavors in this recipe consist largely of onion and rosemary. Other flavor options are garlic, grill seasonings or Asian flavors. See the section on Roasted Tomatoes, page 123 for an extensive list of seasoning ideas.

Place venison in roasting pan or cast iron skillet. Sprinkle with lemon juice and rub in salt and pepper. Cover roast with bacon, tucking in loose ends underneath. Drizzle Worcestershire sauce over covered roast, add onions and rosemary to the pan. Add one cup water to the pan and cover. Bake at 325° 1 to 1 1/2 hours or until a meat thermometer reads 160°, check periodically to ensure liquid has not evaporated, add more liquid if necessary. Remove bacon and let sit 10 minutes before slicing.

INGREDIENTS

- 1 2-3 pound venison roast
- Juice from 1/2 lemon
- 1 teaspoon salt
- 1/2 teaspoon pepper
- 4 slices bacon
- 3 tablespoons Worcestershire sauce
- 2 cups onion, chopped
- 2 sprigs rosemary
- 1 cup water

GARLIC-BLACKENED POT ROAST

Reminiscent of a hearty pioneer-style dinner, pot roast is always a family favorite. The convenience of almost an entire dinner in one pan is an added bonus. Pair this with some homemade corn muffins or flaky rolls and everyone will be satisfied. We love this with moose, and found muskox to be excellent when prepared this way.

INGREDIENTS

- 1 2-3-pound venison roast
- 10 cloves garlic, pureed
- 1/3 cup olive oil
- 1 teaspoon fresh ground black pepper
- 2 sprigs fresh rosemary
- 10 juniper berries, crushed (optional)
- 3 carrots, chopped
- 3 potatoes, chopped
- 2 stalks celery, chopped
- 1 medium onion, chopped
- Salt to taste

In a small bowl, mix garlic, olive oil and black pepper. Place in a sealable plastic bag or airtight container with venison roast, rosemary and crushed juniper berries. Marinate overnight if possible. Remove roast from marinade and salt to taste. Prior to cooking, let marinated venison sit at room temperature 30 minutes. On a hot, cast iron skillet, sear all sides of the roast. Add marinade back to the pan, cover and bake at 350° 45 minutes. Remove cover and turn roast over. Add vegetables and continue to bake, uncovered 45-55 more minutes or until vegetables are tender and roast reads 160° on a meat thermometer. Let sit 10 minutes before slicing.

BBQ SANDWICH

One large crock pot of venison can be the basis of our dinners all week long. This sandwich is one of many meals that are a quick fix from a slow cook. Once cooked, this meat freezes well and can be added to soups, stews or casseroles.

Place venison roast in a large crock pot. Add chopped onion. In a small bowl, whisk remaining ingredients until smooth. Pour over roast and cover. Cook on low heat 6-8 hours. If shredded venison is desired, use two forks to pull roast apart into bite-sized chunks. To enhance flavor, allow to slow cook an additional 15-30 minutes. Place on artisan bread of choice and serve warm. Meat prepared in this way also makes a great baked potato topper or can be served with buttered noodles or rice. Kept warm in the crock pot it is an easy, convenient addition to any potluck.

INGREDIENTS

- 3-4-pound venison roast
- 2 cups onion, chopped
- 1/3 cup brown sugar
- 1/4 cup cider vinegar
- 1 6-ounce can tomato paste
- 2 tablespoons Worcestershire sauce
- 2 teaspoons chili powder
- 2 teaspoons salt
- 1 teaspoon dry mustard

QUICK MEAT & POTATOES

Unbelievably fast, using the pressure cooker tenderizes meat and creates wonderful flavors of a roast that has been slow-cooked all day. Use this recipe as a base and add any of your favorite flavors.

INGREDIENTS

- 2-pound venison roast
- 3 tablespoons vegetable oil
- 4-6 potatoes, peeled
- 5 cloves garlic
- 2 cups beef broth
- 1 cup water
- Salt and pepper to taste

In a pressure cooker, heat oil on medium-high heat. Sear roast on all sides. Add remaining ingredients and cover tightly. Bring cooker to pressure on high heat, reduce to medium and cook 40 minutes, keeping pressure up. Remove from heat and let pressure go down on its own. Remove meat and potatoes from pressure cooker and make gravy using remaining liquid. See Brown Gravy on page 41.

FRENCH ONION VENISON

Easy, easy, easy and a great variation from the standard cream of mushroom soup crockpot meal. We always cook up an extra large batch of this to freeze and use in quick-fix casseroles such as enchiladas and vegetable stir-fries with rice.

If using an older, tougher or gamey roast, marinate in the ingredients at right overnight. If not, put all ingredients in the crock pot and cook on low heat 5-7 hours or until tender. This recipe is great with wild boar and alfalfa-fed deer being placed directly in the crock pot, or bear being marinated. Serve steak style or cube and serve over rice or noodles.

INGREDIENTS

- 3-4-pound venison roast
- 1 cup orange juice
- 1 cup French dressing
- 1 1-ounce package onion soup mix
- 1 large onion, thinly sliced
- 10 whole cloves garlic

VERSATILE VENISON FILLING

With any roast, there is a tendency for leftovers. Usually that is our purpose when choosing to cook a large portion of meat. After we have enjoyed one meal, everyone looks forward to venison sandwiches the next day. Usually, by the next dinner we are ready for the meat to be an addition to something else such as angel hair pasta with a tomato-vegetable sauce, or fajitas loaded with grilled onions, peppers and all the trimmings. This filling can be frozen and added to a dish for a quick meal.

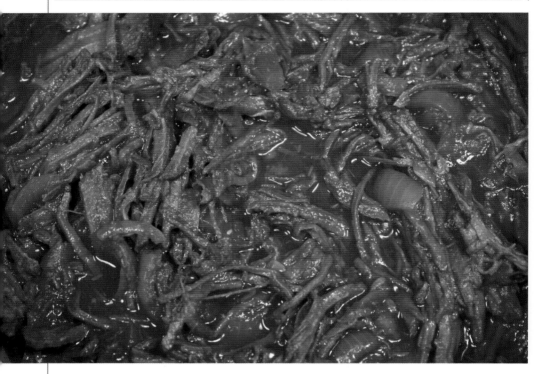

INGREDIENTS

- 3-4-pound venison roast
- 1 15-ounce can condensed tomato soup
- 3 beef bouillon cubes
- 1/4 cup water
- 1 onion, quartered

Place all ingredients in the crock pot and cook on low heat 5-7 hours or until meat is tender and falls apart easily. Add additional seasonings if desired and continue cooking at least 30 minutes to ensure flavor absorption. See Roasted Tomato section on page 123 for a wide variety of seasoning ideas.

BLOODY MARY ROAST

There is more to a good mixer than one may think. Living in Alaska without fresh vegetables for so many years, we became great fans of tomato juice and the many flavors it imparted on our wild-game meals. From pizza to Spanish rice to spaghetti, many dinners were prepared using tomato-vegetable juices as a base. This is one of the easiest and tastiest recipes in the book. The cooked venison can be enjoyed for one meal on its own and added to virtually any dish that requires cooked meat for the next night. We used this repeatedly with caribou over the years.

Place thawed roast in the crock pot. Cover with Bloody Mary mix. Place a foil tent over roast to help retain moisture. Cover and cook on low heat 6-8 hours or until meat is tender. Once fully cooked, roast can be sliced to steak portion sizes with the liquid used as gravy. Venison can be cubed, mixed with sauce and served over rice or pasta, or meat can be shredded to use as sandwich, burrito or meat pie filling.

INGREDIENTS
- 2-3-pound venison roast
- 3 cups Bloody Mary mix

PEPPERED JERKY

Jerky could be considered a food group around our house. Fortunately, for our children, we are always testing out new jerky recipes. No matter what big-game animal we prepare, our family will eat anything that remotely resembles jerky, simply for the smoked flavors.

INGREDIENTS

- 2-3 pounds venison, cut into strips
- 1 quart water
- 1/4 cup Morton Tender Quick or curing salt
- 1/4 cup white sugar
- 1 tablespoon black pepper
- 1/2 tablespoon white pepper
- 2 teaspoons granulated onion
- 2 teaspoons liquid smoke
- 1 teaspoons liquid garlic
- Additional fresh-ground black pepper to taste

When slicing meat for jerky, the traditional cut is in strips that go with the grain. For an easy-to-chew cut, meat can be sliced across the grain. In a large ceramic or glass bowl, mix all brine ingredients with a wire whisk until salt and sugar are dissolved. Add venison, mix thoroughly, and put a plate on top to be sure all meat remains submerged. Soak 8-10 hours, stirring occasionally. Drain brine and remove meat. Do not rinse meat. If additional pepper flavor is desired, grind fresh black pepper on venison at this time. Pat dry or place on racks and let air-dry for up to 1 hour. Follow smoking directions on your smoker. Cooking times vary greatly, depending on make and model of smoker and outside weather conditions. Try to keep the temperature of the smoker between 150° and 200°. Check for doneness after 3 hours. Larger cuts of jerky can be finished on a baking sheet in the oven at 165°, check every 15 minutes. When jerky is done, place in a glass bowl and cover with plastic wrap until cool. Keep refrigerated or freeze if storing for an extended period of time.

SAVORY GARLIC JERKY

Over the years, we have smoked numerous species of game meats taken at various times of the season. From sage-fed muleys to lichen-eating caribou to post-rut elk, this is a great recipe for those who may not be fond of sweet-tasting jerky.

When slicing meat for jerky, the traditional cut is in strips that go with the grain. For an easy-to-chew cut, meat can be sliced across the grain. In a large ceramic or glass bowl, mix all brine ingredients with a wire whisk until salt and sugar are dissolved. Add venison, mix thoroughly, and put a plate on top to be sure all meat remains submerged. Soak 8-10 hours, stirring occasionally. Drain brine and remove meat. Do not rinse meat. Pat dry or place on racks and let air-dry for up to 1 hour. Follow smoking directions on your smoker. Cooking times vary greatly and depend on make and model of smoker and outside weather conditions. Try to keep the temperature of the smoker between 150° and 200°. Check for doneness after 3 hours. Larger cuts of jerky can be finished on a baking sheet in the oven at 165°, check every 15 minutes. When jerky is done, place in a glass bowl and cover with plastic wrap until cool. Keep refrigerated or freeze if storing for an extended period of time.

INGREDIENTS

- 2-3 pounds venison, cut into strips
- 1 quart water
- 1/3 cup Morton Tender Quick or curing salt
- 1 tablespoon brown sugar
- 2 cloves garlic, minced
- 2 teaspoons liquid garlic
- 1 teaspoon granulated garlic or garlic powder
- 1 teaspoon black or white pepper
- 2 teaspoons liquid smoke

HERBAL-INFUSED JERKY

Depending on the season, we have tried many different herb combinations for this recipe. Feel free to change the flavors using what you like or what you have available. Big game does not take on the flavors as readily as smoked fish, and adjustments may be necessary to please your pallet.

INGREDIENTS

- 2-3 pounds sliced venison, cut into strips
- 1 quart water
- 1/4 cup non-iodized salt
- 1/2 cup white sugar
- 2 cups fresh parsley, chopped
- 1 cup fresh cilantro, chopped
- 5-6 sprigs rosemary, chopped
- 2 tablespoons coriander seeds, crushed
- 1 tablespoon dried oregano
- 1 teaspoon white pepper, ground

When slicing meat for jerky, the traditional cut is in strips that go with the grain. For an easy-to-chew cut, meat can be sliced across the grain. In a large ceramic or glass bowl, mix water, salt and white sugar with a wire whisk until salt and sugar are dissolved. Add herbs and spices and combine thoroughly. Add venison, mix, and put a plate on top to be sure all meat remains submerged. Soak 8-10 hours, stirring occasionally. Drain brine and remove meat. Do not rinse meat but take the larger herbs off the meat to prevent bitter flavors. Pat dry or place on racks and let air-dry for up to 1 hour. Follow smoking directions on your smoker. Cooking times vary greatly and depend on make and model of smoker and outside weather conditions. Try to keep the temperature of the smoker between 150° and 200°. Check for doneness after 3 hours. Larger cuts of jerky can be finished on a baking sheet in the oven at 165°, check every 15 minutes. When jerky is done, place in a glass bowl and cover with plastic wrap until cool. Keep refrigerated or freeze if storing for an extended period of time.

SWEET TERIYAKI JERKY

Always the first to go in our house, we can't keep enough of this flavor on hand. It is loved with any kind of wild game and is the first request from our boys when a deer or elk is brought home.

When slicing meat for jerky, the traditional cut is in strips that go with the grain. For an easy-to-chew cut, meat can be sliced across the grain. In a large ceramic or glass bowl, mix all brine ingredients with a wire whisk until salt and sugar are dissolved. Add venison, mix thoroughly, and put a plate on top to be sure all meat remains submerged. Soak 8-10 hours, stirring occasionally. Drain brine and remove meat. Do not rinse meat. Pat dry or place on racks and let air dry for up to 1 hour. Follow smoking directions on your smoker. Cooking times vary greatly and depend on make and model of smoker and outside weather conditions. Try to keep the temperature of the smoker between 150° and 200°. Check for doneness after 3 hours. Larger cuts of jerky can be finished on a baking sheet in the oven at 165°, check every 15 minutes. When jerky is done, place in a glass bowl and cover with plastic wrap until cool. Keep refrigerated or freeze if storing for an extended period of time.

INGREDIENTS

- 2-3 pounds sliced venison, cut into strips
- 3 cups apple juice
- 1 cup teriyaki sauce
- 1/4 cup non-iodized salt
- 1/3 cup brown sugar
- 1 teaspoon garlic juice

BASIC JERKY

Simply put, this is the base for jerky. This recipe allows you to use favorite flavors to create your own signature jerky. Keep salt in mind, as many commercial seasoning blends are 50% or more salt. If this is the case, reduce the amount of curing salt used. The best bet is to use salt-free seasonings, as they pack the most flavor for your money.

INGREDIENTS

- 2-3 pounds venison, cut into strips
- 1 quart water
- 1/4 cup Morton Tender Quick or curing salt
- 1/4 cup white sugar
- 2-4 tablespoons seasoning blend
- 2 teaspoons liquid smoke (optional)

When slicing meat for jerky, the traditional cut is in strips that go with the grain. For an easy-to-chew cut, meat can be sliced across the grain. In a large ceramic or glass bowl, mix all brine ingredients with a wire whisk until salt and sugar are dissolved. Add venison, mix thoroughly, and put a plate on top to be sure all meat remains submerged. Soak 8-10 hours, stirring occasionally. Drain brine and remove meat. Do not rinse meat. If additional flavor is desired, sprinkle more of your favorite seasoning on venison at this time. Pat dry or place on racks and let air-dry for up to 1 hour. Follow smoking directions on your smoker. Cooking times vary greatly and depend on make and model of smoker and outside weather conditions. Try to keep the temperature of the smoker between 150° and 200°. Check for doneness after 3 hours. Larger cuts of jerky can be finished on a baking sheet in the oven at 165°, check every 15 minutes. When jerky is done, place in a glass bowl and cover with plastic wrap until cool. Keep refrigerated or freeze if storing for an extended period of time.

THIS-CAN'T-BE-VENISON MARINADE

If marinating meat longer than 30 minutes, always refrigerate. When using marinade as a basting liquid, remove all meat from marinade and bring marinade to a rolling boil for 3 minutes in order to kill any bacteria. Do not reuse any rub that has come into contact with raw meat. When slow cooking or pressure cooking, cook meat in the marinade. Once venison is cooked, remove from marinade and reduce and thicken remainder as needed to use for flavorful sauces and gravies.

Good friend, top videographer and producer, Ryan Cornish, lives for this marinade. He has made large batches for many people and found it to be very popular. Even people who claim they don't like any type of venison, end up taking seconds of this meat—we found the same to be true. Marinate 2-3 days for optimal flavor and tenderness.

INGREDIENTS

- 1-2 pounds venison
- 1/4 cup real maple syrup
- 1/4 cup soy sauce
- 1/4 cup Worcestershire sauce
- 1/4 cup cider vinegar
- 1/4 cup brown sugar
- 1/4 cup olive oil
- 3-4 cloves garlic, crushed
- 3 sprigs rosemary

GAME-TAMER MARINADE

INGREDIENTS
- 2 cups vermouth
- 1/2 cup white wine vinegar
- 1 onion, minced
- 6 cloves garlic, minced
- 1 tablespoon tarragon
- 2 teaspoons salt
- 2 teaspoons black pepper

STEAK RUB

INGREDIENTS
- 1 tablespoon coarse salt
- 2 teaspoons fresh-ground black pepper
- 2 teaspoons cayenne pepper
- 2 teaspoons paprika
- 2 teaspoons dill weed
- 2 teaspoons ground coriander
- 1 teaspoon garlic powder

DARK AND RICH

INGREDIENTS
- 1 tablespoon coarse salt
- 1 tablespoon coffee, finely ground
- 1 tablespoon dark brown sugar
- 2 teaspoons smoked paprika
- 2 teaspoons granulated onion
- 1 teaspoon fresh-ground black pepper
- 1 teaspoon garlic powder
- 1/2 teaspoon allspice

SPICY RUB

INGREDIENTS
- 2 tablespoons paprika
- 1 tablespoon white sugar
- 2 teaspoons black pepper
- 2 teaspoons salt
- 1 teaspoon chili powder
- 1 teaspoon onion powder
- 1 teaspoon garlic powder
- 1/2 teaspoon cayenne pepper
- 1/2 teaspoon red pepper flakes

CHINESE MARINADE

INGREDIENTS
- 1/3 cup olive oil
- 1/4 cup soy sauce
- 2 tablespoons rice or white wine vinegar
- 2 tablespoons brown sugar
- 2 cloves garlic, minced
- 1 teaspoon white pepper
- 1 teaspoon ground ginger
- 1 teaspoon dry mustard
- 1/2 teaspoon Chinese 5-spice (optional)

TENDERIZING MARINADE

INGREDIENTS
- 1/2 cup red wine
- 1/2 cup Worcestershire sauce
- 1/3 cup olive oil
- 1/3 cup water
- 1 onion, chopped
- 3 stalks celery, chopped
- 4 bay leaves
- 4 cloves garlic, crushed
- 10 peppercorns, crushed
- 8 juniper berries, crushed

TAMING MARINADE

INGREDIENTS

- 1/2 cup oil
- 1/4 cup rum
- 1/4 cup Dijon mustard
- 1/4 cup soy sauce
- 1/4 cup Worcestershire sauce
- 1/4 cup lemon juice
- 4-6 cloves garlic, crushed
- 1 teaspoon black pepper

GAMEY-MEAT MARINADE No. 1

INGREDIENTS

- 1 cup buttermilk
- 1/3 cup lemon juice
- 1 tablespoon garlic powder

GAMEY-MEAT MARINADE No. 2

INGREDIENTS

- 1 cup V-8 juice
- 1/2 cup gin
- 4 stalks celery, chopped

GAMEY-MEAT MARINADE No. 3

INGREDIENTS

- 1 cup apple juice
- 1/2 cup white wine
- 1 tablespoon pickling spices

BEER MARINADE

INGREDIENTS

- 1 cup beer
- 1 tablespoon honey
- 2 teaspoons salt
- 2 teaspoons dry mustard
- 2 teaspoons granulated garlic
- 1/2 teaspoon cayenne pepper

INVENT-YOUR-OWN MARINADE

INGREDIENTS

- 1/4 cup oil
  (olive, grape seed, peanut, canola,
  or vegetable)
- 1/4 cup vinegar
  (cider, balsamic, rice, white or red wine)
- 2 tablespoons soy
  or Worcestershire sauce
- 1 tablespoon sweetener
  (honey, maple syrup, corn syrup,
  molasses, brown or white sugar)
- 1-2 teaspoons each of your favorite
  flavors (up to 3)
- black pepper
- lemon pepper
- red pepper flakes
- granulated garlic
- granulated onion
- dried or fresh herbs

VENISON OR BEEF STOCK

INGREDIENTS

- 4-5 pounds venison or beef bones
- 2 large onions, quartered
- 6 stalks celery, chopped
- 3 carrots, chopped
- 2 large tomatoes, chopped
- 4 cloves garlic, crushed
- 4 bay leaves
- 6 stems fresh parsley
- 10 cups water
- Salt and pepper to taste
- Olive oil (optional)

Place bones in a roasting pan, generously salt and pepper. If using game bones, drizzle with a few tablespoons olive oil. Roast bones at 375° for 1 hour, turning 2-3 times. Place remaining ingredients in a large stock pot and bring to a boil. Reduce heat to low and simmer 5-6 hours. Skim off and discard any fat and foam that rises to the surface. Remove broth from heat and strain. For a richer broth, return strained broth to heat and boil until reduced. Use immediately or cool and freeze for up to 6 months.

*W*ild pigs are the second most hunted big-game animal in North America, behind white-tail deer. Globally, they rate as number one. Living in more countries and island nations than any other big-game species, it's no wonder pork constitutes so much of the world's diet. We've hunted and eaten pigs in several countries, and always look forward to new and exciting ways to cook this meat.

From a pit-smoked pig in New Zealand, where we partook in a traditional Maori feast, to the jungles of Fiji, where, slow-cooked in coconut milk, it served as the main food at a village funeral, to the Australian outback to Indonesia, where the Muslims looked upon us as heathens for eating the flesh, to the rainforest region of Bali, where, served with hot chili peanut sauce it was likely the best-tasting wild pork we've ever had, pigs have provided us with many fond memories. Simply put, wild pig is fun to cook with and is some of the best-eating meat around. Though these recipes are designed for pork, they can be interchanged with many venison and wild turkey meals.

CHILI-ORANGE BRAISED PORK

People are always asking what our favorite recipe is. It's a good question, but when you write cookbooks, that's like asking who your favorite child is; we like them all, otherwise our names wouldn't be behind them. Wild pig is one of our favorite game meats — we've hunted and eaten them in several countries — and one reason is because it easily takes on the flavor of so many different ingredients. We developed this recipe with two of our favorite flavors in mind, and thanks to Great-Grandpa Fountain, an avid 93-year-old gardener who supplied the wonderful red chilies from his garden, and lovely oranges Scott brought back from a hunting trip in California, this recipe is definitely in our top five.

INGREDIENTS

- 2 pounds wild pig stew meat or shoulder roast, cubed
- 2 tablespoons olive oil
- 1/2 cup onion, chopped
- 4 cloves garlic, minced
- 2 cups beef or game stock
- 1/2 cup orange juice
- 2 hot red chilies
- 1 teaspoon orange zest
- 1/2 teaspoon cinnamon
- 1/2 teaspoon dried oregano or 7-10 fresh leaves
- 1/4 teaspoon dried thyme or 5-7 fresh leaves
- Salt and pepper to taste

Lightly season wild boar with salt and pepper. In an ovenproof pan or skillet, heat olive oil on medium-high heat. Add wild pig, brown 3-4 minutes. Add onion and garlic and sauté an additional 1-2 minutes. Add remaining ingredients and bring to a boil. Cover pan and place in a 350° oven. Braise until meat is tender, 40-50 minutes. Serve with bread, rice or pasta, something to soak up the great pan juices.

CAJUN SMOTHERED PORK

Cajun Smothered Pork is one of the most addictive recipes in this entire book. We love the technique of meat covered in vegetables, with enough liquid and flour that after a nice slow cook, becomes gravy. The meat is tender and moist and the roasted vegetables are divine. We actually enjoy this meal with eggs for breakfast, in a sandwich for lunch or at dinner, served with mashed potatoes. This is one you can't get enough of.

Lightly season wild pig with salt and pepper. In a shallow dish mix flour and Cajun seasoning. Dredge wild boar chops in seasoned flour mixture. In a heavy skillet, heat canola oil on medium-high heat. Add wild boar and brown lightly on each side. Remove from skillet and place in a casserole dish. In the same pan, add a bit more oil if needed and sauté onions and peppers 2-3 minutes. Place sautéed vegetables on top of browned chops. Sprinkle remaining seasoned flour over the top, add water and cover. Bake at 350° 40 minutes, checking occasionally, adding additional water if necessary.

INGREDIENTS

- 6-8 wild pig chops, 1/2"-1" thick
- 1/4 cup flour
- 2 tablespoons Cajun seasoning, or Spicy Rub page 58
- 2 tablespoons canola oil
- 1 cup onion, sliced
- 1/2 green bell pepper, sliced
- 1//2 red bell pepper, sliced
- 1-2 jalapeño peppers, seeded and sliced
- 1 cup water
- Salt and pepper to taste

BREAKFAST PORK

A serving of protein starts the day off right, and living in a family of meat-eaters, this is a great recipe that always comes through. Developed to be "kid-friendly", this recipe makes a great alternative to sausage, ham and bacon without any added preservatives.

INGREDIENTS

- 1 pound wild pig, cubed small
- 1 tablespoon real maple syrup
- 1 tablespoon soy sauce
- 1 tablespoon Worcestershire sauce
- 1 tablespoon cider vinegar
- 1 tablespoon brown sugar
- 1 tablespoon olive oil
- 1/4 teaspoon poultry seasoning, or seasoning of choice

Chop wild pig into small cubes, place in a sealable plastic bag or airtight container. Add remaining ingredients and refrigerate up to two days. Heat a skillet on medium-high heat. Add all ingredients to the skillet and fry until desired doneness. Serve with eggs as a side or in an omelet. This recipe also makes a great addition to beans and rice or chili.

PRICKLY PEAR PIG

Known also as nopalitos and pork, this unique dish is a great way to introduce your family to something new. The nopalitos or prickly pear cactus (paddles) can be found in specialty food stores and many grocery stores.

In a large pot, boil wild pig and nopalitos with enough water to cover for 15-20 minutes. Drain and set aside. In the same pot, heat oil and sauté onions until tender. Add garlic and sauté 1-2 more minutes. Add wild boar and nopalitos to the large pot. Add all other ingredients and gently stir. Cover and simmer 20-30 minutes or until wild boar is tender. Remove lid and simmer to desired thickness. Serve with corn chips or warm tortillas. To make this dish in the crock pot, brown meat with onions and garlic, add remaining ingredients and cook on low 4-5 hours or until wild boar is tender.

INGREDIENTS

- 1 pound wild pig, cubed
- 1 1/2 cups nopalitos, sliced bite-sized
- 2 tablespoons canola oil
- 1/2 cup onion, chopped
- 6 cloves garlic, minced
- 1 14.5-ounce can diced tomatoes
- 1 cup corn
- 1 teaspoon dried oregano
- 1/2 teaspoon chili powder

SWEET & SOUR PORK

Slightly intimidated by the intricacies of some Asian cuisine, we found that once we traveled through an area and enjoyed some homemade cooking, we were able to duplicate many of the flavors. This recipe is also great with chicken or turkey.

INGREDIENTS

- 2 pounds wild pig, cubed
- 1/4 cup flour
- 1/4 cup cornstarch
- 4 tablespoons peanut oil
- 1 cup onion, finely chopped
- 4 cloves garlic, minced
- 1 cup bell pepper, chopped
- 1/2 cup carrots, grated
- 8-10 cherry tomatoes, halved
- 1 cup pineapple chunks
- Salt and pepper to taste

Sauce:

- 1/4 cup rice vinegar
- 1/4 cup brown sugar
- 1/4 cup beef broth
- 1/4 cup ketchup
- 2 tablespoons honey
- 2 tablespoons sherry
- 1 tablespoon soy sauce
- 1 tablespoon cornstarch
- 1/2 tablespoon fresh ginger, pureed

In a small bowl, mix all sauce ingredients. Lightly season wild pig with salt and pepper. In a medium bowl, mix flour and cornstarch. Dredge meat cubes in flour-cornstarch mixture. In a heavy skillet, heat peanut oil on medium-high heat. Add wild boar, stir fry 3-4 minutes. Add onion and garlic and continue to stir fry 2-3 minutes. Add carrots and bell pepper, stir fry an additional minute then add sauce mixture. Bring all ingredients to a boil and simmer 20-30 minutes or until meat is tender. Add cherry tomatoes and pineapple during the last few minutes of cooking time. Serve over rice or noodles.

GREAT-GRANDPA'S SAUERKRAUT

This recipe dates back many generations on Scott's Czechoslovakian side of the family. The first "family tradition" recipe Tiffany was subjected to, she was not crazy about it. Strangely, the flavor really grows on you and now she joins the family in eager anticipation whenever someone cooks up a big pot of Grandpa's Sauerkraut & Mush. It is one of those things you can eat all day long.

In a large pot or Dutch oven, fry bacon until crisp. Add wild pig, onions and garlic and cook until meat is browned. Add remaining ingredients, except keilbasa, simmer on low heat until meat is tender.

Add keibasa and cook an additional hour. This recipe also can be cooked in a crock pot on high 3-4 hours. Serve over cornmeal mush or ready-made polenta.

INGREDIENTS

- 2 pounds wild pig, cubed
- 1/2 pound bacon, chopped
- 1 onion, chopped
- 10 cloves garlic
- 1 teaspoon salt
- 1 30-ounce can red kidney beans
- 2 33.8-ounce jars sauerkraut
- 2 pounds keilbasa, sliced

Cornmeal Mush Preparation:

In a medium saucepan, mix cornmeal and salt. Add water and stir. Cook over medium heat until thick and bubbly. Remove from heat and add butter.

Cornmeal Mush:

- 1 cup yellow cornmeal
- 1/2 teaspoon salt
- 2 1/2 cups cold water
- 2 tablespoons butter

YELLOW CURRIED PORK WITH CILANTRO

One of our most memorable curries came while staying in a remote village in Fiji. After hunting wild boar, we returned to share it with others, and came away with new friends and incredible-tasting food. In fact, we enjoy all types of curry flavors are favorites of ours. Depending on the country, or even which region they come from, curries can capture a wide range of flavors. For a quick meal we always have ready-made curries on hand. They can now be found in virtually any grocery store but for a greater variety try an Asian or Indian specialty food store.

INGREDIENTS

- 1-2 pounds wild pig, cubed
- 1 tablespoon peanut oil
- 2 tablespoons yellow curry paste
- 1 tablespoon brown sugar
- 1 teaspoon fish sauce (optional)
- 1 can coconut milk
- 1/4 cup fresh cilantro leaves

Yellow Curry Paste:

- 1 teaspoon cumin seeds
- 1 teaspoon coriander seeds
- 4 dried chilies
- 2 teaspoons yellow curry powder
- 1 teaspoon turmeric
- 1 teaspoon salt
- 1/2 teaspoon ground cloves
- 1/2 teaspoon ground cinnamon
- 2 stalks lemon grass, chop white part only
- 2 shallots, chopped
- 2 cloves garlic, chopped

In a large skillet, heat peanut oil on medium heat. Add yellow curry paste, brown sugar and fish sauce, sauté until bubbly. Add meat to curry mixture and brown. Reduce heat to medium-low and add coconut milk. Simmer, uncovered, 45 minutes or until meat is tender. Remove from heat, add cilantro and serve over rice or noodles.

Yellow Curry Paste Preparation:

Place the cumin and coriander seeds in a pan without adding any oil. Dry-fry them, stirring over medium heat for 1 to 2 minutes until they are slightly browned, and give off a roasted aroma. Coarsely chop the chilies and soak in water for 10 minutes. Drain. Pound all the ingredients together or puree in a food chopper. Refrigerate or freeze unused portion.

PORK & PEA-POD STIR-FRY

When the peas are in the garden we enjoy them almost every day. Why go out for Chinese when you can whip-up this meal in minutes?

Lightly season wild pig with salt and pepper. In a heavy skillet, heat peanut and sesame oil on medium-high heat. Add wild boar, stir fry 3-4 minutes. Add ginger and garlic and stir fry an additional 1-2 minutes. Add soy sauce, honey and pea pods. Continue stir frying until pea pods are bright green. Serve alone, or over rice or noodles.

INGREDIENTS

- 1-pound wild pig tenderloin, cubed
- 1 tablespoon peanut oil
- 1 teaspoon sesame oil
- 2" fresh ginger, minced
- 3 cloves garlic, minced
- 2 tablespoons soy sauce
- 1 tablespoon honey
- 2 cups pea pods
- Salt and pepper to taste

PORK TANGINE

On Tiffany's first trip to Northern Africa, she was overwhelmed with the sights, sounds and smells of a country that was so foreign to her. Finding comfort in a small, brightly colored, family-owned restaurant, she was able to relax and savor some of the world's best cuisine. The joys of sweet and savory, crunchy and soft all come together in this soup-type stew.

INGREDIENTS

- 2 pounds wild pig, cubed large
- 1 tablespoon olive oil
- 1 cup onion, chopped
- 4 cloves garlic, crushed
- 1 teaspoon lemon zest
- 1/2 teaspoon turmeric
- 1/2 teaspoon cumin
- 1/2 teaspoon ginger
- 1/4 teaspoon cinnamon
- 1/4 teaspoon allspice
- 1/4 teaspoon salt
- 1 15.5-ounce can garbanzo beans
- 1/2 cup dried apricots, sliced
- 3 cups chicken broth or turkey stock
- 3 small zucchini, thickly sliced

Lightly season wild pig with salt and pepper. In a heavy skillet, heat olive oil on medium-high heat. Add meat and sear on all sides. Add onion and garlic and continue to sauté 2-3 minutes. Add remaining ingredients and transfer to a tangine or covered baking dish. Bake at 350° 45-50 minutes or until meat is tender. Serve over couscous. An alternate cooking method is a slow simmer on the stove, in a covered pan.

WHITE CHILI

One of the advantages of a career in the outdoor industry is traveling, meeting new people and sharing food secrets. While on a mule deer hunt in South Dakota, Tiffany met Shirley Clarkson, famed cook of Mill Iron Outfitters. Fast friends they became, and after spending an evening over a few pots of chili, she found it hard to spend the next day out hunting when she really wanted to be in the kitchen with Shirley. Although Shirley smokes her pork prior to cooking, and pressure cooks her beans from scratch, this version is a shortcut we hope comes close to doing her fine recipe justice.

Lightly season wild pig with salt and pepper. In an ovenproof pan or skillet, heat butter and olive oil on medium-high heat. Add wild boar, brown 3-4 minutes. Add onion and garlic and sauté an additional 1-2 minutes. Add remaining ingredients except for the lime, and bring to a boil. Reduce heat to low and simmer 1 hour or until pork is tender. This mixture can also be transferred to a crock pot and slow cooked 2-3 hours on low heat. Before serving, squeeze a wedge of lime into each bowl.

INGREDIENTS

- 1-2 pounds wild pig, cubed
- 2 tablespoons butter
- 1 tablespoon olive oil
- 1 cup onion, diced
- 2 cloves garlic, minced
- 2 4-ounce cans diced green chilies
- 1 14.5-ounce can chicken broth
- 2 29-ounce cans pinto beans
- 2 teaspoons Tobasco green pepper sauce
- 1 teaspoon cumin
- 1 teaspoon dried Mexican oregano
- 1/2 teaspoon dried red chili flakes
- 1/4 teaspoon liquid smoke (optional)
- 1 lime, cut into small wedges

HEARTY BARLEY STEW

Perfect for the slow cooker, this recipe takes the work out of a home-cooked meal. Throw it all in and go, in 4-6 hours you have a delicious, healthy stew. Program the bread machine to finish at the same time as the stew and you're set. Sometimes it's just nice to let your appliances do the cooking! Modify this recipe with fresh ingredients if you have the time to chop.

INGREDIENTS

- 1-2 pounds wild pig, cubed
- 1 14.5-ounce can diced tomatoes
- 1 8-ounce can tomato sauce
- 2 4-ounce cans mushroom stems and pieces, undrained
- 1 1/2 cups beef broth or game stock
- 1/2-3/4 cup red wine
- 1/2 cup onion, diced
- 1/2 cup bell pepper, diced
- 1/2 cup carrot, diced
- 1/2 cup celery, diced
- 1/2 cup pearl barley, uncooked
- 3 cloves garlic, minced
- 1 teaspoon salt
- 1/2 teaspoon pepper
- 1/4 cup fresh cilantro
- 1/4 cup fresh parsley
- 1/4 cup fresh basil (optional)

Add everything but the herbs (cilantro, parsley and basil) to a crock pot. Slow cook 4-5 hours on high or 6-7 hours on low or until meat is tender. Add herbs 10-15 minutes before serving.

POT STICKERS

While in China, we enjoyed pot stickers every morning at a traditional breakfast buffet, and it inspired us to make our own. When we pass these around the neighborhood, everyone wants to know when we'll be back with more. A tasty dipping sauce is key; use the one here or an already prepared one such as gyoza sauce.

In a medium bowl, mix the first 7 ingredients until thoroughly blended. Separate wonton wrappers. Use approximately 1 tablespoon of filling for each pot sticker. Spread egg on edges, press and seal. Lay pot stickers individually on a large tray so they don't stick together. Heat canola oil on medium-high heat, fry pot stickers until golden on one side, turn carefully as they tend to stick. Add 1/3 cup water and cover tightly. Steam 3-5 minutes. Serve hot with dipping sauce.

INGREDIENTS

- 1/2 pound ground wild pig
- 1/4 cup fresh cilantro leaves
- 1/4 cup carrot, shredded
- 2 green onion, sliced
- 1 tablespoon soy sauce
- 1 teaspoon sesame oil
- 1 teaspoon ginger root, grated
- 1 beaten egg
- 16-20 square won ton wrappers
- 1-2 tablespoons canola oil

Dipping Sauce:

- 1 tablespoon soy sauce
- 1 tablespoon sambal, or hot sauce of choice
- 1 tablespoon rice vinegar
- 1 tablespoon green onion, sliced

LOCO MOCO

Our favorite Hawaiian fast food, after Spam musubi, is Loco Moco. An ultimate comfort food, this meal keeps you going when you have a busy day of snorkeling ahead of you, or if you want a simple dinner to eat pool-side. Pair this with some of the best fresh fruit the world has to offer and there you have it: paradise. For a shortcut, pre-seasoned sausage patties can be substituted for the meat patty, and ready-made gravy will save time.

INGREDIENTS

Meat Patty:

- 1 pound ground wild pig
- 1 egg
- 1/4 cup bread crumbs
- 2 tablespoons sour cream
- 2 tablespoons ketchup
- 1 teaspoon soy sauce
- 1 teaspoon mustard
- Salt and pepper to taste

Brown Gravy:

- 3 tablespoons butter
- 3 tablespoons flour
- 1 1/2 cups beef broth
- 1 tablespoon Worcestershire sauce
- Salt and pepper to taste

Layer No.1: Rice

Cook 2 cups rice in rice cooker or follow package directions for microwave or stove top.

Layer No.2: Meat Patty

In a medium bowl, mix ingredients for meat patty. If ground wild boar already has added fat, eggs and sour cream can be omitted. Shape into 4-6 round patties. In a preheated skillet, fry patties to desired doneness.

Layer No.3: Fried Egg

Fry 4-6 eggs over easy or sunny-side-up.

Layer No.4: Brown Gravy

In a medium skillet, melt butter on medium-high heat. Stir in flour and whisk until smooth. Lower heat to medium and slowly add beef broth. Cook 5 minutes at a low boil, continually whisking to avoid lumps. Stir in Worcestershire sauce, add salt and pepper to taste.

Assemble Loco Moco by plating all four layers. Finish off with a dash of hot pepper sauce for authentic flavor.

TAMALE PIE

Homemade tamales are one of the gems in Mexican cuisine. They can, however, be quite labor-intensive to create. This is our shortcut, with all the wonderful flavors and none of the extra time. Made ahead of time and refrigerated or frozen, tamale pie can serve a lot of people quickly.

In a large skillet, heat olive oil on medium-high heat. Brown ground pork 3-5 minutes. Add onion and garlic and continue to sauté 2-3 minutes. Add remaining filling ingredients except for the queso fresco. Bring to a boil then reduce heat to low and simmer 20 minutes. Remove from heat, add queso fresco and set aside. In a medium saucepan, mix cornmeal, salt and water. Cook over medium heat, stirring constantly, until thick. Remove from heat and stir in butter. Spread half of the crust mixture into a 9"x13" casserole baking dish. Spoon all filling over bottom crust. Gently spoon remaining cornmeal crust over filling and smooth. Bake at 375° 40-45 minutes. Sprinkle additional grated cheese during last 5 minutes of baking time if desired. Let sit 10-15 minutes before cutting and serving.

Top & Bottom Crust:
- 1 1/2 cups yellow cornmeal
- 1 teaspoon salt
- 4 cups cold water
- 4 tablespoons butter
- Additional grated cheese for topping (optional)

INGREDIENTS
Filling:
- 1 pound ground wild pig
- 1 tablespoon olive oil
- 1 cup onion, finely chopped
- 4 cloves garlic, minced
- 1 cup green bell pepper, chopped
- 1/2 cup red, yellow or orange bell pepper, chopped
- 2 cups corn
- 1 15-ounce can tomato sauce
- 1 14.5-ounce can diced tomatoes
- 1 6-ounce can black olives, sliced
- 1 tablespoon sugar
- 2 teaspoons chili powder
- 1/2 teaspoon cumin
- 1/2 teaspoon black pepper
- 1 1/2 cups queso fresco, crumbled or 1 cup jack cheese, grated

SAUSAGE QUICHE

There is no better one-dish-meal than a quiche, and this version with a potato crust is fantastic. The limitless combinations of meat, vegetables, cheeses, herbs and spices make it a regular "go-to" meal for our family, be it breakfast, lunch or dinner. The fact that quiche can be served hot or cold makes it even more versatile.

INGREDIENTS

- 4 cups fresh or frozen hash browns
- 1/4 cup olive oil
- Salt & pepper to taste
- 1 cup seasoned wild pig sausage (Ground wild boar can be used, season appropriately.)
- 6 eggs
- 2/3 cup milk
- 1/4 cup parsley
- 1/4 teaspoon salt
- 1/2 cup chopped steamed broccoli or asparagus, optional
- 1 cup jack or cheddar cheese, grated

In a heavy skillet, heat olive oil on medium-high heat. Add hash browns and cook until lightly browned. Salt and pepper to taste. Using a large spoon, press hash browns (making a crust) into a greased pie pan. In the same skillet, brown sausage until crumbled, set aside to cool. In a medium bowl, beat eggs with a whisk or electric mixer until frothy. Add parsley and salt. Assemble quiche by sprinkling cooked sausage evenly over hash brown crust, layer vegetables next, pour egg mixture over everything and finish, topping with grated cheese. Bake at 350° 40 minutes or until eggs are set.

SMOKEY MEAT LOAF

Meat loaf is another one of those meals that can be adapted to what is on hand. Growing up we always used crushed soda crackers or bread crumbs. Trying to sneak something different in for our family, grits were a nice addition. Spices can be easily adjusted for individual tastes.

In a large bowl, mix all ingredients until thoroughly combined. Place in a traditional meatloaf pan, a round cake pan or make individual meat loaves using a greased muffin tin. Bake at 350° 30 minutes to 1 hour (cooking time depends on pan selection). Be sure meat loaf reaches an internal temperature of 165°. Serve with salsa if desired.

INGREDIENTS

- 2 pounds ground wild pig
- 1/2 cup quick hominy grits
- 1/2 cup red bell pepper, finely chopped
- 1 4-ounce can diced green chilies
- 2 tablespoons chipotle peppers or jalapeños, minced
- 2 tablespoons dried onion flakes
- 2 tablespoons olive oil
- 2 eggs
- 2 teaspoons chili powder
- 1/2 teaspoon cumin
- 1/2 teaspoon salt

SAGE PLANKED PORK LOIN

Fortunately, for cooking wild game, we have a fresh supply of sage on hand virtually year-round in our herb garden. Thinking of sage as a very strong flavor (when ground) we were hesitant to use it in large quantities. Gradually we have worked our way up to using a lot of fresh sage and find it a wonderful complement to many dishes.

INGREDIENTS

- 2-pound wild pig tenderloin
- 20 fresh sage leaves
- 4 cloves garlic
- 1 tablespoon lemon zest
- 2 teaspoons salt
- 2 tablespoons olive oil
- 1 prepared cooking plank, see page 118

In a food processor or chopper, thoroughly blend sage, garlic, lemon zest, salt and olive oil. Cover pork loin with sage pesto and seal in a sealable plastic bag. Marinate 6-12 hours. Prior to cooking, let marinated wild pig sit at room temperature 30 minutes. Place on a prepared plank, cover with foil, tucking ends of foil 1/2" under plank to seal. Grill or bake at 350° 45 minutes to 1 hour or until desired doneness, 150° (medium-rare) to 160° (well-done). Let sit 10 minutes before slicing.

MEATBALL KEBABS

Meatballs are so versatile, whether preparing them for a main course or an appetizer, they can be used in many ways. They are also a great way to introduce people to wild game due to their sample-size portion. Use suggested vegetables or add fruits or vegetables of choice.

In a small bowl, mix all sauce ingredients. Divide sauce into two bowls, one for basting and one for dipping, set aside. In a medium bowl, mix all meatball ingredients until thoroughly combined. Form into desired meatball sizes. Thread skewers, alternating meat and vegetables, leaving one inch on each end. Place skewers on prepared plank. Brush meat and vegetables with reserved sauce. Grill or bake at 375° 15-20 minutes or until meat reaches an internal temperature of 165°. Baste often. Serve with reserved dipping sauce.

INGREDIENTS

Meatballs:
- 1 pound ground wild pig
- 1 egg, beaten
- 1/2 cup water chestnuts, diced
- 1 tablespoon horseradish
- 1 tablespoon hot mustard
- 1/2 teaspoon salt

Sauce:
- 1/2 cup orange marmalade
- 1 clove garlic, crushed
- 2 tablespoons soy sauce
- 1 tablespoon lemon juice
- 1 tablespoon ginger, minced

Additional Ingredients:
- 1 yellow bell pepper, chopped
- 1 cup mushrooms
- Metal or wooden skewers (soak wooden skewers overnight in water)
- 1 prepared cooking plank, see page 118

ASIAN PLANKED WILD BOAR

After multiple trips to the Australian Outback, where wild pig cooked over an open fire was the norm, the woody flavor was a delight, but more times than not, it could have used a little something extra. The rub and basting sauce in this recipe are flavorful enough to stand alone, but together they make a winning flavor combination. Good hot or cold, this meat can be used as a main course or added to salads and soups.

INGREDIENTS

- 2 pound wild pig roast
- 1 prepared cooking plank, see page 118

5-Spice Rub:

- 1 tablespoon brown sugar
- 1 tablespoon granulated onion
- 1 tablespoon Chinese 5-spice
- 1 teaspoon garlic salt
- 1/2 teaspoon white pepper

Barbecue Basting Sauce:

- 2 tablespoons canola oil
- 1 tablespoon cider vinegar
- 1 tablespoon honey
- 1/2 teaspoon dried thyme
- 1/2 teaspoon allspice
- 1/2 teaspoon smoked paprika

In a small bowl, mix all rub ingredients until thoroughly combined. Wash roast and pat dry. Pierce meat in several places with a fork. Place meat on a plate and massage with rub. Place in a sealable plastic bag and refrigerate at least 8 hours. Prior to cooking, let marinated wild boar sit at room temperature 30 minutes. In a small bowl, mix all basting-sauce ingredients until combined. Place wild pork on a prepared plank, cover with a layer of basting sauce. Grill or bake at 350° 45 minutes to 1 hour or until desired doneness, 150° (medium-rare) to 160° (well-done). Baste often throughout cooking time. Let sit 10 minutes before slicing.

THREE-LAYERED FILLET

Not only is this beautiful dish a show-stopping entree, it is delicious! The stuffing is lighter than a traditional Thanksgiving-type stuffing and makes a great dinner any time of the year.

Prepare pork by dividing the roast into 3 equal sections, lengthwise. Lightly season with salt and pepper. Soak raisins, dates and apricots in rum and hot water. Soak until mixture cools. In a small skillet, sauté onions and garlic in butter until tender. Cool completely. In a medium mixing bowl, combine all ingredients except olive oil. Evenly spread stuffing between two layers of pork, topping with final pork layer. Tie pork loaf together with string. Place pork on greased aluminum foil, drizzle with olive oil and wrap securely. Bake at 400° 50-70 minutes, or until meat thermometer reaches 160°. Baste occasionally with extra virgin olive oil. Let stand 10 minutes in foil before slicing.

INGREDIENTS

- 1 1/2 pound wild pig roast
- 3 tablespoons butter
- 1/2 cup onion, thinly sliced
- 3 cloves garlic, minced
- 1 cup bread crumbs, plain or panko
- 1/3 cup golden raisins
- 1/3 cup dried apricots, chopped
- 1/3 cup dates, chopped
- 2 tablespoons rum
- 2 tablespoons hot water
- 1/4 teaspoon salt
- 1/4 teaspoon black pepper
- 1/8 teaspoon nutmeg
- 1 egg, beaten
- 2 tablespoons extra virgin olive oil
- Salt and pepper

RUBBED & INJECTED PORK ROAST

This marinade is a winner on any wild game and meat can marinate up to 24 hours. The rub can be varied according to individual tastes. We've found this one to be mild, suiting many palates. It can be doubled or tripled and stored for use on steaks and grilled chicken.

INGREDIENTS

- 1 3-5-pound wild pig roast

Injectable Marinade:

- 1/3 cup apple juice concentrate
- 2 tablespoons cider vinegar
- 2 tablespoons Worcestershire sauce

Pork Rub:

- 1 tablespoon brown sugar
- 1 teaspoon garlic powder
- 1 teaspoon onion powder
- 1/2 teaspoon chili powder
- 1/4 teaspoon black pepper
- 1/4 teaspoon salt
- 1/8 teaspoon ground oregano

In a small bowl, mix marinade ingredients. In a small bowl, mix rub ingredients. Place roast in a shallow pan. Using a meat-marinade injector, inject marinade into roast in several places. Generously coat roast with pork rub. Bake at 325° 30 minutes per pound, or until internal temperature reaches 160°. Let sit 10 minutes before slicing.

STUFFED TENDERLOIN

Stuffing a tenderloin is a great way to stretch ingredients to feed more people. Stuffing also helps keep wild game moist and opens up endless flavor opportunities. There is a crispiness to the outside of this tenderloin with a complementary moist interior.

Butterfly tenderloin and pound to 1/2"-3/4" thickness. In a medium bowl, gently mix all stuffing ingredients. Place stuffing evenly over tenderloin. Roll into a log shape and place seam-side down in a greased baking pan. Brush tenderloin with beaten egg and carefully coat with bread crumbs. Bake at 375° 35-40 minutes or until internal temperature reaches 160°. If bread crumbs begin to brown too much, place a foil tent over tenderloin. Let sit 10 minutes before slicing.

INGREDIENTS

- 2-pound wild pig tenderloin

Stuffing:

- 1 1/2 cups crumbled corn bread
- 1/4 cup green olives, chopped
- 1/4 cup sun-dried tomatoes, chopped
- 1/4 cup fresh parsley, chopped
- 1 tablespoon green onion, minced
- 1 tablespoon mustard
- 1 tablespoon extra virgin olive oil

Topping:

- 1 egg, beaten
- 1/3 cup Italian bread crumbs

ORANGE-SOY JERKY

Our motto for jerky, "Never leave home without it!" It's a great source of protein while on hikes and easy to eat with a fishing pole in one hand. This slightly sweet version is very popular with the kids, and of all the jerky we make, wild pig is probably our favorite.

INGREDIENTS

- 2-3 pounds wild pig, cut into strips
- 3 cups water
- 3/4 cup orange juice
- 1/2 cup white sugar
- 1/4 cup Morton Tender Quick
- 1/4 cup soy sauce
- 1/2 tablespoon granulated onion
- 1/2 tablespoon garlic powder
- 1 teaspoon white pepper (optional)

When slicing meat for jerky, the traditional cut is in strips that go with the grain. For an easy-to-chew cut, meat can be sliced across the grain. In a large ceramic or glass bowl, mix all brine ingredients with a wire whisk until tender quick and sugar are dissolved. Add wild pig, mix thoroughly, and put a plate on top to be sure all meat remains submerged. Soak 8-10 hours, stirring occasionally. Drain brine and remove meat. Do not rinse meat. If additional pepper flavor is desired, sprinkle white pepper on wild boar at this time. Pat dry or place on racks and let air-dry for up to 1 hour. Follow smoking directions on your smoker. Cooking times vary greatly and depend on make and model of smoker and outside weather conditions. Try to keep the temperature of the smoker between 150° and 200°. Check for doneness after 3 hours. Larger cuts of jerky can be finished on a baking sheet in the oven at 165°, check every 15 minutes. When jerky is done, place in a glass bowl and cover with plastic wrap until cool. Keep refrigerated or frozen if storing for an extended period of time.

5-SPICE JERKY

Most people can't quite put their finger on the flavors in this jerky recipe. The Chinese 5-spice enhances the flavor of wild boar in a truly unique way.

When slicing meat for jerky, the traditional cut is in strips that go with the grain. For an easy-to-chew cut, meat can be sliced across the grain. In a large ceramic or glass bowl, mix all brine ingredients with a wire whisk until Tender Quick and honey are dissolved. Add wild pig, mix thoroughly, and put a plate on top to be sure all meat remains submerged. Soak 8-10 hours, stirring occasionally. Drain brine and remove meat. Do not rinse meat. Pat dry or place on racks and let air-dry for up to 1 hour. Follow smoking directions on your smoker. Cooking times vary greatly and depend on make and model of smoker and outside weather conditions. Try to keep the temperature of the smoker between 150° and 200°. Check for doneness after 3 hours. Larger cuts of jerky can be finished on a baking sheet in the oven at 165°, check every 15 minutes. When jerky is done, place in a glass bowl and cover with plastic wrap until cool. Keep refrigerated if storing for an extended period of time.

INGREDIENTS

- 3 pounds wild pig, cut into strips
- 1 quart water
- 1/4 cup honey
- 1/4 cup soy sauce
- 2 tablespoons Morton Tender Quick
- 1 tablespoon Chinese 5-Spice
- 1 tablespoon granulated garlic
- 1/2 tablespoon white pepper

If marinating meat longer than 30 minutes, always refrigerate. When using marinade as a basting liquid, remove all meat from marinade and bring marinade to a rolling boil for 3 minutes to kill any bacteria. Do not reuse any rub that has come into contact with raw meat.

ASIAN TANG MARINADE

Wine may be substituted for vinegar in this recipe, add fresh ginger for a more intense flavor.

INGREDIENTS
- 1/4 cup honey
- 1/4 cup red wine vinegar
- 2 tablespoons soy sauce
- 2 tablespoons sesame oil
- 4 cloves garlic, minced
- 1 teaspoon ginger
- 1 teaspoon dry mustard
- 1 teaspoon hot pepper sauce (optional)

Mix all ingredients in a sealable plastic bag. Marinate 30 minutes to overnight. Grill, bake or stir fry meat.

SWEET APRICOT MARINADE

Adding jams and jellies to marinades is a wonderful way to add a sweet power punch. Try going a bit more exotic and add guava or passionfruit jelly to this marinade.

INGREDIENTS
- 1/3 cup apricot jam
- 1 tablespoon coarse salt
- 2 teaspoons fresh-ground black pepper
- 2 teaspoons cayenne pepper
- 2 teaspoons paprika
- 2 teaspoons dill weed
- 2 teaspoons ground coriander
- 1 teaspoon garlic powder

Mix all ingredients in a sealable plastic bag. Marinate 30 minutes to overnight. Grill, bake or stir-fry meat.

TAMARIND MARINADE

Don't be afraid to try tamarind, it is one of the distinguishing ingredients in Worcestershire sauce and worth looking for in your supermarket in the Asian or Hispanic food sections.

INGREDIENTS
- 1/2 cup rice vinegar
- 4 tablespoons tamarind paste
- 4 green onions, chopped
- 2 cloves garlic, crushed
- 1 jalapeño chili, chopped
- 1 tablespoon fresh mint, finely chopped
- 1 teaspoon chili powder
- 1/4 teaspoon ginger

Mix all ingredients in a sealable plastic bag. Marinate 30 minutes to overnight. Grill, bake or stir fry meat.

INDIAN RUB

There are many great Indian recipes that work nicely as side dishes. Try this rub with venison, too, and grab a jar of mango chutney, some jasmine rice and your favorite dal, you'll have an authentic Indian feast in no time.

INGREDIENTS
- 1/2 teaspoon salt
- 1/2 teaspoon ground cumin
- 1/2 teaspoon ground coriander
- 1/2 teaspoon fennel seeds, crushed
- 1/4 teaspoon white pepper
- 1/4 teaspoon turmeric
- 1/4 teaspoon cinnamon
- 1/8 teaspoon ground cloves

In a small bowl, mix all ingredients. Rub into chops or cubed wild pig. Sauté or grill accordingly.

ACHIOTE RUB

Annato seeds also make a great flavored oil. When preparing to sauté a dish, first sauté annato seeds in olive oil and watch the beautiful color appear. Discard seeds and continue cooking.

INGREDIENTS

- 2 tablespoons annatto seeds
- 1 tablespoon warm water
- 1 teaspoon cumin seeds
- 1 teaspoon ground oregano
- 1 teaspoon allspice
- 1 teaspoon salt
- 4-6 garlic cloves
- 3 tablespoons lime juice
- 1/2 teaspoon lime zest

Soak annatto seeds overnight in 1 tablespoon water. In a food chopper or blender, thoroughly mix soaked annatto seeds and remaining ingredients forming a paste. Cover meat and roast in the oven or plank cook on the grill.

QUICK MOLE SAUCE

Mole comes in so many variations we don't think we have ever tasted the same mole twice. It provides a unique flavor and will liven up any dish.

INGREDIENTS

- 1 clove garlic
- 1 tablespoon olive oil
- 1 small onion, minced
- 1 can tomato paste
- 1 teaspoon fresh oregano
- 1 tablespoon dark chili powder
- 1 teaspoon cumin
- pinch allspice
- pinch salt
- 1/2 oz unsweetened chocolate

In a food processor or chopper, thoroughly blend all ingredients. Add to stir-frys or add 1 can of beef broth for a stewing liquid.

GREEN SAUCE

Fresh flavors make up this light, tangy sauce. Great cooked with meat on served salsa style.

INGREDIENTS

- 1 cup tomatillos, finely chopped
- 1 cup fresh cilantro
- 1/4 cup onion
- 1 jalapeño, seeds removed
- 4 cloves garlic
- Juice and zest of 1/2 lime

In a food processor or chopper, thoroughly blend all ingredients. Add to stir-frys, rice and pasta dishes.

*T*he simple mention of eating bear meat turns the noses of many people. Fact is, properly cared for and cooked, it's some of the best-eating meat in North America. We gave one of the following recipes, along with four others—two elk, a deer and a pronghorn—to five different taste-testers, leaving it a mystery as to what kind of meat they were eating. All but one of the testers rated the bear as their favorite; you should have seen their faces when they learned it was bear!

The following recipes were tested alongside many types of venison, and very few people were able to pick out the bear. Bears are omnivores, and black bears, especially, yield great meat. We've eaten all three bears, polar, grizzly and black, and prefer the black, simply due to its highly vegetative diet. Give it a chance, and you'll soon understand why they are fast becoming one of the most popular big-game animals in the country.

STEAKS, STRIPS & CUBES

STEWS & SOUPS

GROUND

PLANKED

ROASTS & FILLINGS

JERKY

MARINADES & RUBS

STROGANOFF

Our oldest son was very excited to cook up "Daddy's bear." Although he can be a picky eater, he is usually willing to try any type of wild game. Not being a fan of anything in a creamy sauce, we were pleasantly surprised when Braxton went for his third serving. Interestingly, it was a big old boar, taken in the spring.

INGREDIENTS

- 2-3-pound bear roast
- 1 envelope (1-ounce) onion soup mix
- 1 10.5-ounce can cream of mushroom soup
- 2 tablespoons ketchup
- 1 tablespoon mustard
- 2 4-ounce cans sliced mushrooms
- 1 cup sour cream

Cut roast into 4-6 large chunks. Lay in the bottom of a crock pot or slow cooker. Sprinkle onion soup mix evenly over meat. Cover meat with cream of mushroom soup. Cover and cook on high heat 3 hours or until meat is very tender. Cut meat into bite-sized chunks, turn crock pot to low. Add ketchup, mustard and sliced mushrooms mixing carefully. Cook an additional hour. Before serving, add sour cream and warm. Serve over wide egg noodles and garnish with parsley.

BEAR PITA

The first time we had a traditional pita with hummus and tzatziki, while traveling through Europe, was a memorable experience, one we wanted to bring home. The amazing spices and flavors compensated for the fact we had no idea what kind of meat we were eating. Later we learned it was goat. We've since had it with both black bear and grizzly, and both were excellent.

In a small bowl, combine all ingredients. Marinate bear in refrigerator up to 24 hours. Heat a medium skillet on medium-high heat, add bear with all marinade. Bring to a quick boil, letting marinade reduce, 5-10 minutes. Strain off marinade and discard. Serve bear in a warm pita with lettuce, tomatoes, hummus and tzatziki.

Tzatziki:
- 1 cup Greek yogurt or sour cream
- 2 cups cucumber, diced
- 4 cloves garlic, minced
- 1 tablespoon extra virgin olive oil
- 2 teaspoons vinegar or lemon juice
- 1 teaspoon dill weed (optional)
- Salt and fresh ground black pepper to taste

Dice cucumbers and place on several paper towels. Pat dry to remove extra water. In a medium bowl mix all ingredients. Keep refrigerated.

INGREDIENTS
- 1 pound bear, cut into small chunks
- 1/3 cup fresh lemon juice
- 1/4 cup olive oil
- 4 cloves garlic, pureed
- 1 teaspoon fresh thyme, finely chopped
- 1 teaspoon fresh marjoram, finely chopped
- 1 teaspoon fresh ground black pepper

Hummus:
- 1 15-ounce can garbanzo beans, drained
- 3 tablespoons tahini
- 2 cloves garlic
- 2 tablespoons fresh lemon juice
- 1 tablespoon extra virgin olive oil
- 1/2 teaspoon cumin
- Dash of cayenne or hot sauce

Place all ingredients in a food chopper and puree until smooth. Keep refrigerated.

HONEY BEAR WITH FRIED RICE

When looking for creative ways to use leftovers, think casseroles, soups, stews and stir-frys.
Cooking meat in big batches is also a time-saver and once cooked and cooled, seasoned meat can be
frozen as well.

INGREDIENTS

- 1 pound cooked bear meat, cubed
- 3 cups cooked rice
- 2 tablespoons canola oil
- 2/3 cup corn
- 2/3 cup edamame or peas
- 1/2 cup carrots, sliced

Honey Sauce:

- 1/4 cup cider vinegar
- 3 tablespoons honey
- 2 tablespoons soy sauce
- 2 tablespoons ketchup
- 2 teaspoons fresh ginger, minced (optional)

In a small, bowl thoroughly combine sauce ingredients, set aside. In a large wok or skillet, heat oil on medium-high heat. Add vegetables and stir-fry 1-2 minutes. Add rice and sauce, stirring gently. Lastly, add bear and cook until hot throughout or bear cubes reach an internal temperature of 165°.

BEAR & BROCCOLI

Believe it or not, the secret ingredient in this recipe is coffee. Coffee enhances the flavor of the meat and creates a rich dark sauce. This quick stir-fry is also great with with deer, elk and antelope.

Marinate bear in coffee and sugar overnight. In a large wok or skillet, heat peanut oil on medium-high heat. Stir-fry shallots and garlic 3-4 minutes. Add bear cubes and thoroughly brown, 5-8 minutes. Add ginger and continue cooking 1-2 minutes. Add remaining ingredients, turn heat to medium-low, cooking 20-30 minutes or until meat is tender. In a separate pot or container, steam broccoli and add right before serving. Serve with rice or green tea soba noodles.

INGREDIENTS

- 1 1/2 pounds bear, cubed
- 2 cups strong coffee
- 1/4 cup sugar
- 2 tablespoons peanut oil
- 1/3 cup shallots, thinly sliced
- 4 cloves garlic, thinly sliced
- 1 tablespoon ginger, minced or pureed
- 2 tablespoons soy sauce
- 1 teaspoon toasted sesame oil
- 1/2 teaspoon Chinese 5-Spice
- 2 cups broccoli, steamed

BBQ BEAR CHUNKS

In our family, the end pieces of many meats such as ribs and roasts are the first to be gobbled up. This recipe cooks the meat down so that every piece tastes like a caramelized chewy "end-piece." We had no trouble eating every bite and no one got poked with a fork! For a shortcut, use prepared barbecue sauce. It is the method here that makes the dish what it is and the flavors greatly accentuate the meat, be it a spring or fall bear.

INGREDIENTS

- 2 pounds bear, cut into bite-sized chunks

Sauce:

- 2 tablespoons butter
- 1 onion, diced
- 1 bell pepper, diced
- 2 cloves garlic, minced
- 1 cup apple juice
- 1/2 cup cider vinegar
- 1/2 cup ketchup
- 2 tablespoons Worcestershire
- 2 tablespoons molasses
- 1 teaspoon dry mustard
- 1 teaspoon salt
- 1 teaspoon pepper
- 1 teaspoon chipotle hot sauce (optional)

In a medium sauce pan, melt butter on medium-high heat. Sauté onions until translucent. Add peppers and garlic and sauté an additional 3-5 minutes. Add all other sauce ingredients and bring to a boil. Turn heat to low, taste and adjust seasonings if desired. Continue to simmer sauce while bear bakes. Place bear chunks in an oven-proof casserole dish. Bake in a preheated 350° oven, 30 minutes. Drain liquid and fat from bear meat. Cover meat with BBQ sauce and continue cooking an additional hour. Serve with black beans and rice.

PASTRY-TOPPED LENTIL SOUP

Many fans of the bear meat will tell you that once you've had good bear you'll take it over venison most of the time. We agree, and this is one of those recipes that, if you're a nonbeliever, will convince you that bear meat is one of the most underrated big-game meats in the country.

In a large stew pot or Dutch oven, brown ground bear on medium-high heat. Once crumbled, add onions, shallots and garlic. Sauté until onions are tender. Add celery, carrots, jalapeño pepper and continue sautéing 3-4 minutes. Add lentils and broth and bring to a boil. Reduce heat to low and simmer uncovered, 30 minutes. Add vinegar, mustard, parsley, salt and pepper to taste. Spoon into individual ovenproof soup bowls. Top each bowl with a square of puff pastry. Make a few slits in the top for steam to escape. Bake at 400° 15-20 minutes or until pastry is golden brown.

INGREDIENTS

- 1 pound ground bear
- 1 cup onions, diced
- 1/4 cup shallots, diced
- 4 cloves garlic, minced
- 1 cup celery, diced
- 1 cup carrots, diced
- 1 jalapeño pepper, diced
- 1 1/2 cups lentils, any color
- 6 cups beef broth or stock
- 2 teaspoons cider vinegar
- 2 teaspoons spicy brown mustard
- 1/4 cup fresh parsley, chopped
- Salt and pepper to taste
- 8-10 5x5 squares puff pastry

BEAR STEW

There is nothing better to come home to, especially after a cold day afield, than a steaming bowl of stew with fresh biscuits. To add another layer of flavor, prior to cooking, bear can be marinated in any of the marinades mentioned in this chapter.

INGREDIENTS

- 2 pounds bear, cubed
- 3 tablespoons vegetable oil
- 1/2 cup flour
- 1/2 cup onion, diced
- 4 cloves garlic, minced
- 3 cups beef broth
- 1/2 cup red wine
- 1/4 cup teriyaki sauce
- 1 15-ounce can tomato sauce
- 1 14.5-ounce can diced tomatoes
- 1 cup celery, chopped
- 3 cups cabbage, thinly sliced
- 1 large potato
- 2 carrots
- 6 bay leaves
- 1 teaspoon celery seed
- Salt and black pepper to taste

Salt and pepper bear cubes. Dredge cubes in flour, coating all sides, set aside. In a large stew pot or Dutch oven, heat vegetable oil on high heat. Add floured bear and brown 5-7 minutes. Add diced onion and garlic. Continue to sauté 2-3 minutes. Add any leftover flour and sauté 5 more minutes. Add remaining ingredients, cooking 5-10 more minutes or until stew comes to a boil. Reduce heat to low. Continue to simmer on the stove 2 hours, or place in crock pot or slow cooker on high 2-3 hours or until bear is tender.

BEAR SAUSAGE WITH MUSTARD SAUCE

GROUND

Mediterannean flavors dominate this sausage giving it a light, fresh taste. These are terrific in a sandwich but can also be made into bite-sized patties to be served as appetizers. Those unfamiliar with bear seem to be more open to small samplers at first.

If possible, grind bear, pork and oatmeal in a grinder with a medium plate. Bear, pork and oatmeal can also be mixed in a large bowl, by hand. In a small saucepan, heat olive oil on medium-high heat. Sauté onions and garlic until tender, remove from heat and cool completely. Combine all ingredients and shape into desired patties. Fry in a nonstick skillet or with a small amount of olive oil or butter until juices run clear or meat thermometer reads 165°. Serve with mustard sauce.

INGREDIENTS

- 1 pound ground bear
- 1 pound plain pork sausage
- 1/2 cup oatmeal
- 3 tablespoons olive oil
- 1 cup onion, minced
- 2 cloves garlic, minced
- 3 tablespoons fresh parsley, chopped
- Juice and zest from 1/2 lemon
- 1 egg
- 1 tablespoon vinegar
- 1/2 teaspoon pumpkin pie spice
- 1/4 teaspoon cayenne pepper
- 1 1/2 teaspoons salt

Mustard Sauce:

- 2 tablespoons mayonnaise
- 1 tablespoon Dijon mustard
- 2 teaspoons parsley, minced
- 1 teaspoon lemon juice
- 1/4 teaspoon white sugar
- 4-6 dashes hot pepper sauce

SMOKEY MAPLE BEAR SAUSAGE

Making sausage is a fun experience both for the versatility and for the creativity that goes into it. Our kids love anything with a maple flavor so even if we add something green to this sausage, they will still eat it.

INGREDIENTS

- 2 pounds ground bear
- 1 pound bacon, ground
- 1 tablespoon maple flavoring
- 2 teaspoons red pepper flakes (optional)
- 1 teaspoon poultry seasoning
- 1 teaspoon black pepper
- 1 teaspoon salt
- 1/2 teaspoon coriander
- 1/2 teaspoon liquid smoke (optional)

Chop bacon into 1" pieces and grind the above ingredients in a grinder until thoroughly mixed. Ingredients can be mixed with a food chopper but take special care not to puree the meat. Shape into desired patties. Fry in a nonstick skillet or with a small amount of olive oil or butter, until juices run clear or meat thermometer reads 165°.

CHEESY BEAR MEAT LOAF

Meat loaf comes in many shapes and sizes at our house. From standard loaf pans, to cake pans to bunt pans to free-formed patties on a plank, we have fun with our meat loaf. This recipe is a great "first-time-bear" recipe for both the cook and the guests.

Mix all ingredients until thoroughly combined. Place in a loaf pan or an 8" x 8" casserole dish, bake at 350° 45 minutes to 1 hour or until internal temperature reaches 165°.

INGREDIENTS

- 1 1/2 pounds ground bear
- 1 egg
- 1 6-ounce can tomato paste
- 1/4 cup milk
- 1/2 cup onions, finely chopped
- 1/2 cup bread crumbs
- 2 cloves garlic, pureed
- 1 teaspoon Italian seasoning
- 1 teaspoon dry mustard
- 1/2 teaspoon red pepper flakes (optional)
- 1/2 teaspoon salt
- 1/4 teaspoon black pepper
- 1/2 cup mozzarella cheese, 1/2" cubes
- 1/4 cup parmesan cheese, grated

GORGONZOLA MEAT PUFFS

This recipe is delicious with any ground meat, as the strong cheese flavor complements the taste of the meat. Leftover meat loaf can be substituted for the cooked bear sausage. Those not fond of gorgonzola or blue cheese can use another cheese such as feta or ricotta.

INGREDIENTS

- 1 cup cooked bear sausage
- 1/2 cup gorgonzola or blue cheese
- 1/2 cup fresh spinach, finely chopped
- 15-20 5x5 squares puff pastry, cut diagonal

In a small bowl, mix cooked bear, cheese and spinach. Place 1 tablespoon mixture onto a phyllo triangle and fold, making a smaller triangle. Seal edges with water or beaten egg. Bake at 400°, 15-20 minutes or until golden brown. Serve warm. Garnish with additional cheese if desired.

PLANKED KEBABS

Planked kebabs are nice in that the wood catches a lot of the juices that would normally be lost into the grill. The flavorful essence of the wood used is very complementary to bear meat. We suggest using cedar or hickory cooking planks for this recipe.

In a small bowl, mix all marinade ingredients. Place marinade and bear chunks in a sealable plastic bag, refrigerate overnight. Remove meat from marinade and thread onto skewers leaving one inch on each end. Place skewers on prepared plank. Brush meat lightly with oil. Grill or bake at 375°, 15-20 minutes. Serve kebabs with a wedge of lime.

INGREDIENTS
- 2 pounds bear, cut into chunks

Marinade:
- 1/2 cup soy sauce
- 1/4 cup olive oil
- 2 tablespoons brown sugar
- 2 tablespoons fresh ginger, minced
- 4 cloves garlic, minced
- 1 tablespoon chili powder
- 2 teaspoons cumin
- 1 teaspoon pepper
- Juice and zest from 1 lime
- Olive or canola oil for basting
- Metal or wooden skewers (soak wooden skewers overnight in water)
- 1 prepared cooking plank, see page 118

PLANKED BEAR AND ONIONS

Many people have a preconceived notion that bear meat is not palatable. Perhaps it's due to their view that these creatures are meat-eating predators. Fact is, black bears are omnivores, typically eating considerably more plants than they do meat. The result, some of the best-eating meat nature has to offer.

INGREDIENTS

- 2 pounds bear, strips
- 2 Walla Walla onions, sliced
- 2 tablespoons olive oil
- 2 tablespoons white vinegar
- 2 tablespoons Worcestershire sauce
- 2 tablespoons real maple syrup
- 1 teaspoon salt
- 1/2 teaspoon black pepper
- 1 prepared cooking plank, see page 118

Mix all ingredients in a large bowl or sealable plastic bag. Refrigerate overnight. Drain all marinade and discard. Carefully place one layer of onions on prepared cooking plank. Place bear strips atop onion layer. Top with remaining onions. Grill or bake at 375°, 25-30 minutes or until meat reaches desired doneness. Stir meat and onions occasionally to ensure even cooking.

TEX-MEX FILLING

This meat filling can be catered to fit any tastes. Use a favorite prepared or homemade salsa be it hot or mild, add heat with jalapeños or add a favorite taco, burrito or fajita seasoning instead of chili powder and cumin. This recipe suggests using a pressure cooker, but a slow cooker can also be used, high heat 6-8 hours.

In a pressure cooker, heat oil on medium-high heat. Sear bear roast on all sides. Add salsa and tomato sauce and seal pressure cooker lid (or follow manufacturer's instructions). Once pressure cooker has reached at least 15 pounds pressure (or started to rock) on high heat, set timer for 40 minutes. Reduce heat to medium or just enough to keep pressure constant. Remove and let pressure come down naturally as meat is still cooking. When pressure is released, open lid and tear meat with fork, add spices. Keep warm until ready to fill burritos, tacos, enchiladas or use as a salad topper. This filling can be frozen up to three months.

INGREDIENTS
- 2-3-pound bear roast
- 2 tablespoons canola oil
- 2 cups salsa or picante sauce
- 1 cup tomato sauce or V-8
- 2 teaspoons chili powder
- 1 teaspoon cumin
- 1 teaspoon hot pepper sauce

BEAR UNDER PRESSURE

Unbelievably fast, using the pressure cooker tenderizes meat and creates the wonderful flavors of a roast that has been slow-cooked all day. Use this recipe as a base and add any of your favorite flavors.

INGREDIENTS

- 2-pound bear roast
- 3 tablespoons vegetable oil
- 2 onions, quartered
- 10 cloves garlic
- 2 cups beef broth
- 1 cup water
- Salt and pepper to taste

In a pressure cooker, heat oil on medium-high heat. Sear roast on all sides. Add remaining ingredients and cover tightly. Bring cooker to pressure on high heat, reduce to medium and cook 40 minutes, keeping pressure up. Remove from heat and let pressure go down on its own. Remove meat from pressure cooker and make gravy using remaining ingredients or make Brown Gravy on page 41. Serve with boiled potatoes.

BEAR ROAST WITH GRAVY

We first tried this recipe on polar bear while living in Alaska, and it works well on grizzly and black bear as well. Pot roasting is an easy way to prepare dinner. With very little preparation and fuss, a tender, melt-in-your-mouth meat results with this slow, moist-heat cooking method. Add vegetables during the last 45 minutes of cooking time if desired.

Coat roast with seasoned flour. In a heavy skillet, heat oil on medium-high heat. Sear all sides of roast and transfer to a baking dish. Add liquid to baking dish, cover and bake at 325°, 1 to 1 1/2 hours or until meat thermometer reaches 170°. Turn roast occasionally. Thicken pan drippings with water and cornstarch for gravy if desired. Let roast sit 10 minutes before slicing.

INGREDIENTS

- 3-5-pound bear roast
- 1/4 cup seasoned flour
- 2 tablespoons canola oil
- 2 cups beef broth, red wine or water

BEAR JERKY

All of the venison and wild-pig jerky recipes can be applied with bear. The only change made for bear meat is to add a bit more seasoning and always more garlic. One of the most important steps when making bear jerky is letting it sufficiently air-dry. For the best outcome, do not skip this step.

INGREDIENTS

- 3-4 pounds bear, cut into strips
- 1 quart water
- 1/4 cup Morton Tender Quick or curing salt
- 1/2 cup brown sugar
- 1 tablespoon black pepper
- 1/2 tablespoon white pepper
- 2 teaspoons granulated onion
- 2 teaspoons liquid smoke
- 1 teaspoons liquid garlic
- 6 juniper berries, crushed
- 6 whole allspice, crushed
- Additional fresh-ground black pepper to taste

When slicing meat for jerky, the traditional cut is in strips that go with the grain. For an easy-to-chew cut, meat can be sliced across the grain, and bear meat, being large-grained, simply melts in your mouth when cut this way. In a large ceramic or glass bowl, mix all brine ingredients with a wire whisk until salt and sugar are dissolved. Add bear meat, mix thoroughly, and put a plate on top to be sure all meat remains submerged. Soak 8-10 hours, stirring occasionally. Drain brine and remove meat. Do not rinse meat. If additional pepper flavor is desired, grind fresh black pepper on bear at this time. Pat dry or place on racks and let air-dry for up to 1 hour. Follow smoking directions on your smoker. Cooking times vary greatly and depend on make and model of smoker and outside weather conditions. Try to keep the temperature of the smoker between 150° and 200°. Check for doneness after 3 hours. Larger cuts of jerky can be finished on a baking sheet in the oven at 165°, check every 15 minutes. When jerky is done, place in a glass bowl and cover with plastic wrap until cool. Keep refrigerated or frozen if storing for an extended period of time.

If marinating meat longer than 30 minutes, always refrigerate. When using marinade as a basting liquid, remove all meat from marinade and bring marinade to a rolling boil for 3 minutes to kill any bacteria. Do not reuse any rub that has come into contact with raw meat.

SPICE TRADE RUB

INGREDIENTS

- 1 tablespoon granulated onion
- 2 teaspoons salt
- 2 teaspoons thyme
- 1 teaspoon black pepper
- 1 teaspoon allspice
- 1/2 teaspoon cayenne pepper
- 1/2 teaspoon cinnamon
- 1/4 teaspoon nutmeg
- 1/4 teaspoon ginger

GREEK RUB

INGREDIENTS

- 2 teaspoons lemon zest
- 2 teaspoons fresh-ground black pepper
- 2 teaspoons dried thyme
- 1 teaspoon salt
- 1 teaspoon ground sage
- 1 teaspoon garlic powder
- 1 teaspoon rosemary, finely chopped

BEAR-TAMER MARINADE

INGREDIENTS

- 1/2 cup cider vinegar
- 1/2 cup apple juice
- 6 bay leaves
- 4 cloves garlic, crushed
- 20 whole peppercorns
- 10 whole allspice
- 10 whole cloves
- 1 teaspoon salt

WILD BEAR MARINADE

INGREDIENTS

- 1 cup vermouth
- 1 cup onions, chopped
- 1/2 cup canola oil
- 1/4 cup white wine vinegar
- 4 cloves garlic, chopped
- 1 teaspoon tarragon
- 15 peppercorns, crushed

SMOKEY BBQ RUB

INGREDIENTS

- 2 tablespoons smoked sweet paprika
- 1 tablespoon brown sugar
- 1 tablespoon sea salt
- 1 tablespoon cumin
- 1 tablespoon chili powder
- 3 teaspoons fresh ground black pepper
- 1 teaspoon cayenne pepper (optional)

CITRUS MARINADE

INGREDIENTS

- 1/4 cup orange juice
- 1/4 cup lemon juice
- 1/4 cup soy sauce
- 1/4 cup brown sugar
- 18-ounce can pineapple chunks
- 4 cloves garlic, minced
- 4" fresh ginger, minced
- 1 tablespoon orange or lemon zest
- 1 teaspoon white pepper

EASY-TAMING MARINADE

INGREDIENTS

- 1 cup milk
- 8 cloves garlic, crushed
- 4 stalks celery, finely chopped

Game Care & Preparation

aximizing the taste of wild game is a multi-step process, and begins well before heading afield. From having the proper tools to field-dress game to having ample freezer space at home, there is a wide range of responsibilities hunters must consider in order to ensure quality meat is retained from the animals being taken.

In some cases however, no matter how prepared you are, the finished product may not be improved upon from what you start with. In other words, the flesh of an old, tough animal can't compete against that of a young specimen of the same species. Then again, we've had some very good eating meat of old animals — an ancient boar black bear taken in the spring rivaling the taste of any wild game we've tried anywhere in the world.

The diet of animals can also impact the flavor of the meat, namely sage and bitter forages. A big buck taken from the high desert that's been feeding on sage may have a stronger taste to it, often being mislabeled as *"gamey."* On the other hand, a deer taken from an alfalfa field could well produce the best, most tender venison ever tasted. An animal's diet can influence the taste of its flesh.

Then there are the factors of what the animal itself is doing at the time of being taken. For instance, some hunters refuse to shoot animals on the run, believing that a buildup in lactic acid and drop in glycogen results in tough meat. Others claim a head shot animal that dies quickly, turns out the best-tasting meat. Still others, primarily those seeking quality meat, refuse to take mature animals during the rut, when hormone levels are high, physical activity is maxed and body fat content low. All of these are good points, but to say each is 100% accurate all of the time would be misleading.

We can't clarify as to why some particular animals taste better than others, only that we've eaten excellent deer and elk taken in the peak of the rut, after the rut, and at various times of the hunting season. One year, an early season head-shot doe pronghorn was among the worst we'd ever eaten, while an old, smelly buck in rut was about the best we'd had of that species. Conversely, a handful of animals we've

taken on the run have proven to be very good eating. Conclusion: it is what it is; some animals simply taste better than others, for many reasons which may forever remain a point of contention among hunters.

That said, there are certain measures to take to ensure the quality of meat, so taste and texture are maximized in the end. Following is a rundown of what can be done to help keep your meat as fresh and tender as possible, no matter what the animal may have been eating or what time of year it was taken.

■ FIELD DRESSING

Before any shots are fired at game animals, be sure of the target. That is, make sure the animal appears healthy, not sick in any way. With Chronic Wasting Disease being a concern in some parts of the country, it's a good idea to wear rubber gloves when field-dressing game, to prevent the spread of bacterial growth and contracting disease. If hunting in regions with recorded Chronic Wasting Disease exposure, avoid consuming the spleen, lymph nodes and eyes, or even handling the brain and spinal cord.

Once an animal is down, the quicker it can be cleaned, or field-dressed, the better. Quickly dressing an animal ensures the cooling process can start, as loss of body heat is the objective in order to prevent deterioration of the meat by gut contents entering the flesh. Not only is immediate field-dressing a good idea, especially on hot days, but boning the meat is also wise.

Typically, on hot days when we can't get an animal into a cooler, we bone out a large majority of the game we take while in the field. When dealing with big animals like elk and moose, even bears, their leg bones are big, and can retain lots of heat. First, place the animal on its back, remove the hide, then start quartering the animal. Once the four quarters are removed, then bone-out the meat to make sure it quickly cools. This is particularly important on early season hunts when daytime temperatures can be very hot.

If not wanting to bone your meat, then, once the quarters are off, hang them in the shade of a tree to start cooling. With all four quarters removed and cooling, extract the backstrap, and hang it to cool. Last, remove the neck and ribs, then retrieve the tenderloins from inside the body cavity.

When boning meat, separate the muscles as evidenced by the silver lining of tissue that divides them from other muscles. This takes time in the field, but evens out when doing the final butchering back home.

Once boned, the meat can be placed inside game bags and hung to further cool. Not only will boning result in meat cooling quickly, but its very clean and retards against the meat contacting any gut content.

If field-dressing an animal and desiring to keep it whole through the aging process, make certain the knife is continually cleaned, to prevent gut content from coming into contact with the meat. To dress an animal, lay it on its back, front end slightly elevated. Spread the hind legs and make an incision from the anus to the sternum. Using the knife handle and free hand, push the guts down while lifting the skin to cut the hide, whereby avoiding risk of puncturing the stomach.

Next, cut around the anus, loosening the entire rectum so it will come out with the rest of the guts. Cut the diaphragm free from the rib cage, then reach up inside and sever the windpipe, heart, lungs and connective tissues of any blood vessels. Pull the guts out of the animal, either from the side or out the back, between the hind legs. Make certain the rectum is removed, then lift the animal from the head, so blood will drain out this cavity. If alone, and working with big animals, dump excess blood out the side.

Hang the animal by the head (or legs, if this is the position it was in when you removed the hide) to start cooling, then wipe the inside cavity of any blood. At this time, what you do with the hide depends on outside temperature and whether or not the pelt would be best left on for transport. If choosing to remove the hide in the field, be sure to keep as much hair as possible from contacting the meat, as hair is dirty and often transmits foul tastes. Once done, wipe down the hanging carcass and cut out all bloodshot damage. We like doing a final wipe-down of a skinned carcass with a vinegar-water solution, at a ratio of one cup vinegar to two quarts water.

If you plan on staying afield, and temperatures are cool enough, it's ideal to leave the hide on the animal, covering it with a game bag. This prevents the meat from drying out, keeps it clean and free of insects. If leaving the hide on an animal to age, remove the windpipe and open the neck, as the thick hide and heavy muscles in this region retain a great deal of heat. Safe temperature ranges to keep the hide on an animal are considered to be from 40 degrees or less. On fat animals such as bear, it's wise to remove the hide as quickly as possible, no matter what the temperature.

Try not to let the carcass freeze before rigor mortis has a chance to set in, as this can toughen the meat. However, it's not an end-all if meat does freeze before you can get it processed. Several of the animals we took while living in the Alaskan Arctic froze solid before we could get their skins off. When it's 40 below zero and the winds are howling, even big animals freeze rapidly. When this happened — and it happened with Dall sheep, caribou and moose — we'd simply quarter the animals with hide intact, then, once home, would thaw it out. Once thawed, we'd butcher the meat and freeze. Refreezing big-game meat is not as taboo as many people tend to believe; it's not like fish which carries a high water content and may get mushy.

If the air temperature is too warm, above 40°F, remove the hide and cover the carcass with a game bag. Better yet, keep the hide on the animal for transportation, and get the animal to a cooler as quick as possible. If air temperature is above 50°F, it's suggested to get the carcass in a cooler within three to four hours of being killed, or as soon as possible.

If camping on your hunt, and you know it's going to be warm with the likelihood of not getting your animal to a cooler until a day or two after being taken, take along several bags of ice. This ice can either be placed inside the body cavity of the animal, or the meat can be boned and placed in coolers of ice — we prefer the latter. Quick cooling is the key to good-tasting meat.

■ AGING MEAT

Aging meat is the practice of holding cuts of meat or an entire carcass of an animal at temperatures between 34° to 37°F for up to fourteen days. The purpose of aging is to allow enzymes in the meat to break down some of the more complex proteins present in the carcass, resulting in tender, flavorful meat. However, not all meat should be aged.

If it's too warm, do not risk aging the meat, especially if it was not properly cooled. To do so is to risk contamination of both the meat and yourself. If the carcass holds little or no fat, aging is not recommended, for the meat can dry out too much and these carcasses are more susceptible to deterioration through microbial breakdown, or spoiling. Young animals need not be aged for extended periods, as their meat is already tender.

When aging meat, it's best to leave the hide on the carcass, to prevent drying out of the meat and considerable weight loss. Of course, this is based on attaining the optimal temperature range mentioned above. If cooling a carcass in a freezer where humidity levels are high, it's best to remove the hide to prevent spoilage.

If aging a carcass with the hide removed, do not trim any fat from the carcass. Fat serves to protect the meat and prevents excessive moisture loss. However, once aged, trim the fat away, as fat carries with it undesirable flavors.

The question of whether or not to age meat, let alone for how long, has always been a point of debate among hunting circles. Some of the conclusions are based on geographic settings being hunted, as well as times of year. They're all valid points, but ask any professional butcher, and you'll see there's no substitute for making meat taste better than through proper aging.

It's best to keep meat aging, again, between the 34° to 37°F temperature mark, for seven to 14 days. If conditions permit and you can make it to ten days, you'll really notice the benefits of aging. Better yet, if you can make it to 14 days, you'll ask yourself why you've ever eaten anything but wild game that's properly aged. After 14 days of aging, tenderness slows down considerably, so there's little reason to go beyond this timeframe.

If meat is to be ground into sausage or burger, aging is not necessary as the grinding process tenderizes the meat. In fact, if grinding your meat, do so as soon after taking the animal as possible, to minimize moisture loss and spoilage.

Aging meat is not for everyone, and if you have reservations, butchering and freezing an animal as quickly as possible is an option. In fact, freezing meat is perhaps the most accepted way to maintain its quality. Some people claim, and rumored studies have supported this, that quickly freezing meat results in breaking down the flesh, whereby making it tender, thus serving a similar purpose as aging by way of hanging.

Some longtime hunters and meat processors we know suggest that if not desiring to age your meat, at least wait up to 12 hours prior to freezing it. This is the time it takes most meats to reach the state of rigor mortis, a process where muscle tissue stiffens. If meat is frozen prior to rigor mortis setting in, the pH will remain too high and the meat will have poor flavor and be tough.

When hunting in freezing conditions, try not to let the meat freeze prior to rigor mortis setting in. If having to remove the hide, take measures to keep the meat from freezing solid. One suggestion is to cover the meat in plastic then cover with snow to insulate from freezing. If this can be done until rigor has set in, the final product will taste better.

■ BUTCHERING

Butchering your own meat is easy, and I'm happy to say that in the many years our families have been involved in hunting, we've never taken an animal to the butcher, electing to do it on our own. Point is, if we can do it, so can you. It's fun and rewarding. Is it perfect every time? No. It doesn't have to be. As long as you know the basic cuts, that's all that's necessary in retaining your own meat via self-processing.

We've butchered everything from Dall sheep to moose, bears to rabbits, and not only does this save money, but leaves no question as to the meat you are preparing. If you do choose to go to the butcher, and there are many great ones out there, make certain they keep your meat separate from that of other customers, especially in this day and age of Chronic Wasting Disease and Hairloss Syndrome.

If doing your own home butchering, there are some basic food-safety measures we suggest. As with other high-protein foods, wild game must be carefully handled in the

VENISON *Cuts*

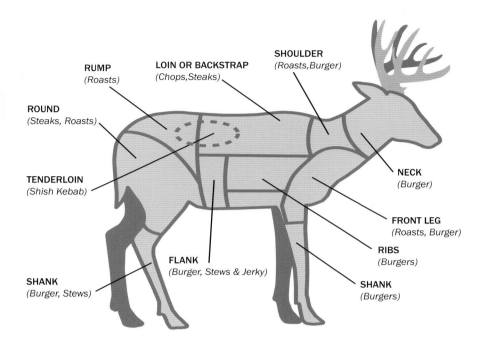

RUMP
(Roasts)

LOIN OR BACKSTRAP
(Chops, Steaks)

SHOULDER
(Roasts, Burger)

ROUND
(Steaks, Roasts)

TENDERLOIN
(Shish Kebab)

NECK
(Burger)

FRONT LEG
(Roasts, Burger)

RIBS
(Burgers)

FLANK
(Burger, Stews & Jerky)

SHANK
(Burgers)

SHANK
(Burger, Stews)

WILD PIG *Cuts*

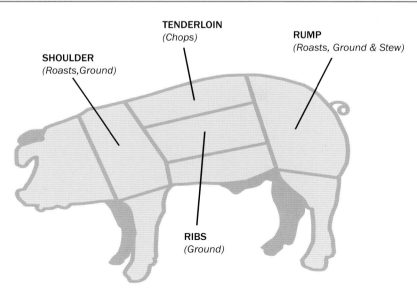

TENDERLOIN
(Chops)

RUMP
(Roasts, Ground & Stew)

SHOULDER
(Roasts, Ground)

RIBS
(Ground)

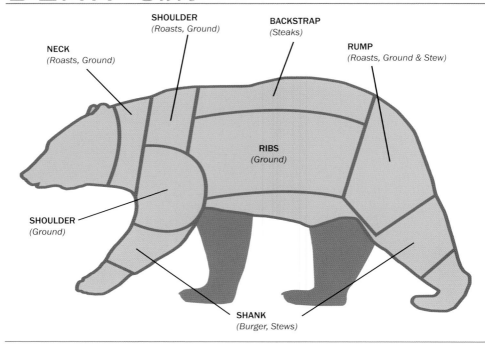

NECK
(Roasts, Ground)

SHOULDER
(Roasts, Ground)

BACKSTRAP
(Steaks)

RUMP
(Roasts, Ground & Stew)

RIBS
(Ground)

SHOULDER
(Ground)

SHANK
(Burger, Stews)

kitchen. Bacteria and other microorganisms can be spread through a kitchen via several sources, from hands to tools to countertops. Here are some recommendations which will help reduce the risk of contracting food-borne illnesses.

- Begin with clean equipment, and once used, thoroughly wash with hot, soapy water.

- Thoroughly wash hands with soap and water before beginning to work. If changing tasks, especially from cutting meat to something else, wash hands each time.

- When done, wash cutting boards and equipment with hot, soapy water. Further sanitize these items with a solution of 1 tablespoon chlorine bleach per one gallon of water. Spray or wipe the solution and let items air-dry.

- When cutting raw meat to cook, even if it's been frozen, do so on a cutting board separate from what salads, vegetables and other foods will be prepared on.

When butchering your own meat, break it down into body parts. Separate the pieces into quarters—both front and hind—backstraps, tenderloins, neck and ribs. Have a bowl on-hand for hamburger or jerky pieces you come across during the butchering process.

The front shoulder is easy to work with, and comes off the carcass by cutting beneath and all the way around the shoulder blade, following the neck line. There are no bones to cut through or maneuver around, meaning a front shoulder is simple to remove. Trim out the shank for burger or sausage. The larger muscles can be separated from the shoulder blade and arm bones. On larger animals, a shoulder roast will be obtained, as will generous supplies of meat for jerky, stew and pieces for other uses. Some of the shoulder meat can be rolled and tied together with string, providing a boneless shoulder roast.

A good portion of meat comes from the hind quarter. To remove the hind quarter, cut close to the spine and work your way down the front side of the leg, toward the shank. Carry the cut all the way around the leg, as close to the skeleton as possible. Articulate the knife into the ball joint, which will free the leg from the carcass.

When boning-out the hind quarter, start the cut on the inside of the leg, near the ball joint. Continue along the leg bone itself, working the muscle away from the femur, all the way down to the knee joint. Separate the big muscles, which are easy to differentiate based on their being encapsulated by the silver skin linings. Be sure to remove this silver skin, for even when it's cooked, this can add considerable toughness to the meat.

Several steaks and roasts will be derived from a hind quarter. The leftover meat, as well as the shank, can be used for burger, stew pieces, sausage and jerky.

Removing the backstrap is the easiest, and considered by many to be the most tasty part of any wild game. Starting at the base of the neck, where the backstrap dives into the neck muscles, simply cut along the backbone, down to the ribs, all the way to the hind quarter. You can stop a bit shy of the hind quarter, which offers a separate rump roast. Now make another cut, from the front side, against the ribs themselves. This cut will join the first cut made along the length of the spine, making for easy removal of the entire backstrap.

Once removed, clean the backstrap of all fat and sinew. Finally, cut the sections of meat into desired loin, steak and stir-fry size.

Inside the body cavity is the tenderloin. These can be quite small, but we consider them to be the tastiest, most tender cuts of meat on all big game. The tenderloins lay adjacent to one another against the spine, just in front of the start of the hind quarters. By making a cut along the front and back edges, tenderloins are easily removed. Wash them of any blood and gut content and slice into medallions to be cooked as desired. This is our favorite cut to savor while on the hunt, over an open campfire.

At this point, all that remains for butchering the animal is the neck, flank and rib meat. Articulate the meat from the bones in these regions, being sure to remove fat and any sinew material. This meat is best used for grinding into burger, but can also make good jerky and stew pieces on larger game.

◼ STORAGE

Once the meat has been prepared into desired cuts, it's time to store it. This is an important step, for you've come this far, you don't want to risk losing the meat to freezer burn. Be sure and use a quality wrapping material, such as waxed freezer paper, heavy aluminum foil, plastic wrap, polyethylene bags or a combination thereof. We'll often wrap the meat in plastic wrap first, then follow it up with a layer of freezer paper, or go with a double layer of freezer paper. For long term storage, nine months or longer, vacuum sealing is a good way to go. If wrapped well so no air can get in, meat will keep for a surprisingly long time; we've kept it for over two years with no problem.

To attain the best quality of meat, freeze when it's in good condition. Be sure all fat, blood, blood vessels containing coagulated blood and hair are removed from the meat prior to freezing. When freezing the meat, select portion sizes corresponding to the family/meal size you'll be cooking for. If unsure, it's better to wrap two smaller packages than one big one, whereby having to refreeze extra meat.

During the wrapping process, be sure to squeeze all the air from around the meat, as this trapped air is what causes freezer burn. For optimal preservation, it's ideal to have your freezer set at 0°F or lower.

When finished wrapping, be sure to label each package with the species, cuts and date. This will allow you to keep track of the meat you have stored, and is especially important if you take multiple animals each year, whereby allowing you to rotate through back-stock.

As you freeze your packaged meat, lay it out individually on the freezer shelves, to allow cold air to circulate around the package and quickly freeze the meat. Avoid placing piles of wrapped meat into the freezer, for it may take several hours for the meat in the center to freeze solid. Once the meat is frozen, it's a good idea to place the packages inside cardboard boxes. Not only does this help you organize your meat by species and/or cuts, but maximizes freezer space as more packages can be stacked on one another and are easier to get at.

Prior to amassing a large quantity of game meat, say from multiple animals, check specific state hunting regulations. Some states require that all wild game be used up before the next hunting season. Make sure as to the amount of game you can keep and for how long you can keep it.

*W*hen it comes to game meats, most people have a story. Many of them go something like: *"My mom cooked venison one way only, dry and tough; I still can't stand the smell of it!"* Or, *"I always use my mom's venison recipe, it's great but my family is tired of the same ol' condensed cream of mushroom soup in the crock pot dinner."*

In this book you will learn ways to cook venison that will change your opinion of wild game. Wild game is a delicacy to many people and cultures, which explains why it's on the menu of so many five-star restaurants.

Slow-cooking tops the list when it comes to maximizing the flavor and tenderness of cooking wild game. But in our fast-paced society, people are turning to more convenient, faster food. However, fast food does not have to mean compromising nutritional value and flavor. With a little preplanning and specific considerations, you can bring wild game to your table quickly, in a unique and delicious fashion.

■ KEEP IT MOIST

One of the many reasons we are such fans of wild game is because lean meats are unquestionably more healthful. Moist-heating methods are preferable to dry ones if trying to keep wild game meals low-fat. However, if you desire to grill, roast or broil your game, be prepared to put some fat back into the meat before, during and sometimes after the cooking process.

Covering meat in foil will help with moisture retention. Replace fat by using bacon, salt pork or cooking oils. Meat can also be rubbed with butter or margarine, beef suet or covered in sour cream. Fat can be added both inside and outside of a rolled roast before roasting. Keep ground-meat dishes moist by adding an egg or sweet or sour cream.

Basting meat throughout the cooking duration will also help keep meat moist. When turning meat on the grill, use tongs, not a fork which can pierce the meat and cause valued juices to escape.

■ MEAT THERMOMETER

If you do not have a meat thermometer, invest in one soon if wishing to maximize wild-game cooking efficiency. Because venison tends to cook faster than beef, many people accidentally overcook it. There is also the common misconception that just because meat was raised in the wild the *"gaminess"* has to be *"cooked out."* This leads to an overcooked, dry product that often gives wild game a bad rap. Honestly, after subsisting off wild-game meat for over a decade, we feel store-bought meats have more mysterious components than wild game we shot and butchered ourselves. Bottom line, a meat thermometer can be your best friend when cooking wild-game.

On the next page is a chart of common cooking temperatures. Through experimentation you will discover how you prefer different cuts of meat to be cooked. Another useful hint, simply looking at a cut of meat can be an indicator as to its doneness. The meat should be cooked until it's no longer pink and the juices run clear.

Venison Roasts and Steaks

- Medium Rare 145°
- Medium 160°
- Well Done 170°
- Ground venison, sausage or jerky 160°
- Casseroles, stuffed fillets, meat loaf, reheated leftovers (including soups and stews) 165°

Wild Boar

- Medium Rare 150°
- Medium 155°
- Well Done 160°
- Ground or stuffed 165°

Bear

- Medium 165°
- Well Done 170°
- Ground or reheated leftovers 165°

cooking on the edges. Cook microwave-thawed meat immediately.

If unthawing ground venison or sausage, periodically take it out and remove the unthawed portion. Return the frozen portion and repeat this step. With any cuts that may have an extra gamey taste, marinate them while unthawing. For instance, frozen steaks or stew pieces can be placed in a few cups of milk during the entire thawing period, whereby significantly reducing the gamey taste. We relied on this method while living in Alaska, and it works well on bear and wild boar, too.

Be sure to clearly label all packages, so you know what you're working with before you begin cooking with it. For example, if you have a mule deer taken in the rut, label it as such. At the same time, if you have an early season moose, make a note of the date it was taken. This little step will aid in the cooking process, starting the moment you begin unthawing the meat.

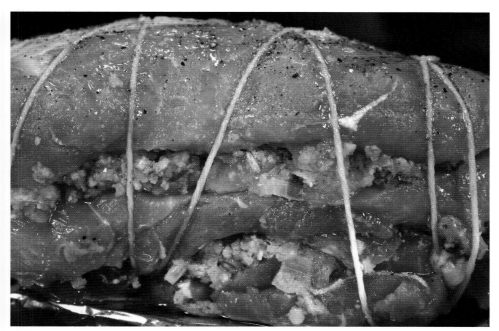

Be sure to cooke stuffed meats longer to ensure doneness.

■ Thawing

For the best flavor and consistency, thaw frozen meat in the refrigerator. Place meat in a shallow pan to prevent dripping on other foods. Wild game can be thawed in the microwave but turn it often to prevent meat from

■ Marinading

Tenderizing, enhancing flavor and disguising gamey flavors are a few of the many benefits marinades can do for wild game. Because of the low fat content of most wild game, the marinades we use are almost always oil-based.

If they are not oil-based, then oil is used elsewhere in the cooking process.

Keep salt use to a minimum while marinading, it has a tendency to dry out the meat and prevent proper browning. The flavor issue can be solved by adding salt right before or during the cooking process.

If marinating meat longer than 30 minutes,

Many of the same techniques in preparing domesticated game apply to wild game, pounding, cubing and grinding all help tenderize tough cuts of meat. Grinding is beneficial simply for the versatility offered as well as the option to add equal parts wild game to ground beef, ground pork or ground turkey .

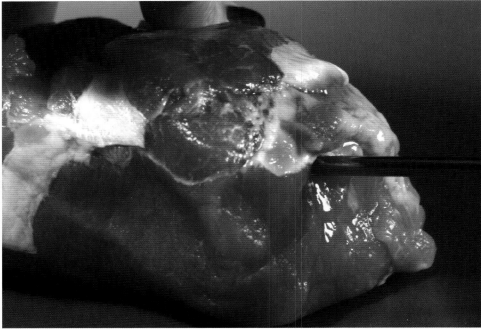

For large cuts of meat and more flavor throughout, use a meat syringe to inject marinade.

always refrigerate. Cover container with a well-sealed lid and occasionally rotate meat. Sealable, plastic bags work well for marinade, just be sure to remove most of the air from the bag. Although sealed, it's a good idea to place these bags in a shallow dish, just in case of a spill. Turn bags frequently and/or massage marinade into meat to help with flavor absorption. Marinade can even be vacuum sealed into meat using bags or containers. This is a great way to cut down on marinading time.

If possible, do not reuse marinade once it has touched raw meat. Save a portion of the marinade prior to marinating to use as a basting or dipping sauce. If marinade that has touched meat is to be used as a basting sauce, bring to a rolling boil for at least 3 minutes and cool to warm before basting. Reduce marinades by half for a rich, flavorful sauce.

Grinders not only grind and tenderize meat, they are instrumental in making your own sausage, and most come with attachments to meet a range of cooking techniques.

■ COOKING METHODS

There are two basic methods to cooking meat, dry and moist heat. When cooking with dry heat, roasting, broiling or stir-frying, be sure there is substantial fat used. Grilling can be a challenge since there is no way to retain the natural juices of the meat. We've found that a quick dredge through extra virgin olive oil when placing steaks on the grill aids in moisture retention. Also follow the general rules of grilling and only turn the meat once. Another great way to retain moisture when grilling is to cook the meat on a plank.

When roasting, use the tips mentioned in Keep It Moist, page 114, to add fat to meat. When broiling, add fat and baste frequently. Finishing the meat with a pat of butter is an easy and elegant way to add fat and flavor to a lean cut of meat. When stir-frying or pan broiling, heat oil in the pan and cook meat quickly over high heat.

Braising is easy and tenderizes any cut of meat.

Pour it in and go, crock pot cooking is the easiest of all methods.

Moist heat is the more common method for cooking wild game and less tender cuts of other meats. Braising is a personal favorite of ours and a wonderful way to add many layers of flavor to your dish. The meat can be seasoned before or at the time of searing. More flavor can be added with the liquid and the sauce, or pan drippings can be jazzed-up for a wonderful gravy. The best part about braising, is popping it in the oven and walking away. Just be sure the liquid never evaporates. Stewing follows the same low and slow principles as braising with the crock pot or stove top being good mediums of preparation. In both braising and stewing, meat is always cooked well done and fork-tender.

The process of plank cooking dates back to early Native Americans. This style of cooking results in tender, juicy foods and can be used on any type of game or fish.

When it comes to keeping game meat moist, it's tough to beat a plank, which also infuses delectable flavors.

■ THERE ARE THREE EASY-TO-FOLLOW STEPS TO PLANK COOKING

STEP No.1 Soak plank in water or suggested liquid, minimum 1 hour, maximum 24 hours.
STEP No.2 Preheat plank on grill at medium heat 5 minutes or in a 350° oven 10 minutes.
STEP No.3 Brush a light coating of olive oil onto cooking side of plank.

There are three cooking options when using a plank. Methods are chosen for flavor, time and/or convenience.

GRILL (DIRECT HEAT):

Use the lowest setting on a gas grill or low charcoal heat. Place plank with food directly over the heat source. Cook with the lid closed so smoke surrounds food and infuses flavor.

Plank should reach heavy smoke in 15-20 minutes. When plank begins to smoke, check often—use spray bottle filled with water to extinguish any flame on the plank. This method promotes a heavy smoke flavor. Grill temperature should be 400°-500°.

GRILL (INDIRECT HEAT):

Use a medium setting on a gas grill. If using charcoal, pile coals to one side. Place plank opposite the heat source. Cook with lid closed so smoke surrounds food and infuses flavor. Plank should begin to smoke after 15-20 minutes. The plank should not catch fire using this method. Cooking time increases due to the lower temperature. This method promotes a light smoke flavor. Grill temperature should be at least 350°.

OVEN:

Preheat oven and plank to 350° or as stated in recipe. Place plank with food, directly on oven rack. Position a foil-lined baking sheet on the rack below the plank to catch any drippings. This method infuses a light smoke essence into food. Planks can be cleaned and reused.

When plank cooking we highly recommend using a thermometer to check for grill temperature.

◾ WARNING

When plank cooking, never leave planks unattended. Avoid repeatedly opening grill cover as this can cause flare-ups and lost heat. When opening grill, take caution not to inhale or stand in direct smoke.

Suggested woods for wild game are alder, apple, cedar, cherry, hickory, maple and oak. Planks can be purchased as oven or grill planks or can be bought in a lumber yard and cut to desired size. Always make sure the wood used is untreated and non-resinous. For a complete recipe guide on plank cooking, check out our book, *Plank Cooking*, available from Frank Amato Publications and select stores nationwide.

◾ SMOKING TIPS

The process of smoking meats is simple; the fats are drawn out while sealing in the flavor. The combination of heat and smoke break down the fibers within the meat, while simultaneously releasing fats. The result is a tender piece of cooked meat packed with flavor. The longer the meat is exposed to heat, the drier it becomes. The more dry a piece of venison, pig or bear, the longer it can be stored.

No matter what recipe is applied, the goal in attaining a well-textured piece of smoked meat lies in creating a balance between salt, sugar, smoke and heat. Adding other spices and flavors is a great way to come up with your own signature blend.

Wood chips and chunks add a great deal of flavor variety. Some of our favorites for smoking are apple, alder, cherry, hicory and pecan chips.

■ Kitchen Appliances and Cookware

When cooking is a passion, it seems the need for various kitchen appliances and cookware never ends. Even if cooking is not a favorite pastime, investing in a few kitchen appliances will have you cooking more efficiently. My first must-have item when dealing with big game is a slow-cooker or crock-pot. There are many great slow-cooking appliances on the market, some that can go from stove top to crock pot mode, some that will brown or sear the meat prior to cooking the meat and traditional Dutch ovens that can be covered with briquettes and left to cook in camp. With a little preplanning, slow cooking is a great way to have dinner ready in ten minutes or less.

The second most used appliance in our home is a smoker. We have run the smoker gamut, from homemade smokers to mini models like the Little Chief, large versions such as the Traeger pellet-fed BBQ/Smoker, and efficient, easy smokers like the Bradley that is fed by bisquettes. All have their place, and often which you choose to use comes down to personal preference. We like them all.

Other appliances worth mentioning are pressure cookers, indoor and outdoor grills, grinders, deep-fryers and food choppers. All of these appliances have a place in our kitchen

and are well used. They all make preparation and cooking time much more efficient.

Cookware plays a role in cooking wild game due to the techniques being used, such as braising or stir-frying, and the presentation of the final product. One of our favorite presentations using specialized cookware is the Moroccan tangine. The cookware is not only decorative but it serves a purpose in the way food cooks. Ceramic cookware used in braising keeps an even heat and presents nicely at the table. Nonstick pans are useful when dealing with very lean cuts of meat and sausage.

Stainless-steel cookware is great when wanting to sear or brown meat using high heat and later gather the brown tidbits left behind, in order to enhance sauce or gravy. Most brands can go from stove top to oven for convenient braising.

Wood cooking planks are considered cookware in our household. Used mainly for the flavor they infuse into foods, we also enjoy serving right off the plank. They are so versatile they can even be used as an "odor-blocker" when cooking strong-smelling foods such as fish. Many types of wood can be used and planks come in many shapes and sizes.

Cast-iron cookware is still a favorite in our kitchen, there are days when every meal is prepared in the same pan. The more cast iron is used the better it becomes and when well seasoned can almost function as a non-stick pan. If planning to cook outdoors, investing in a good Dutch oven is a great place to start. We use both the heavy cast iron and the revolutionary hard-anodized models. Since the hard annodized is so lightweight we use it indoors on the stove and in the oven. The even heat distribution cannot be beat when cooking wild game.

When it comes to preparing wild game, there are certain steps which can be taken to optimize your efforts. Be it saving time or money, being prepared and creative can go a long way in turning out a great dish. Resourcefulness and personal awareness are good starting points, and these are easier to manage than one might think. Following are pointers that have helped us-learned through many years of trial and error—maximize our time, cut costs and produce fine-eating wild game.

■ MAKING SUBSTITUTIONS

Living in Alaska's Arctic, there were no neighbors from whom to conveniently borrow a cup of sugar. Well, they may have had a cup of sugar but they likely would not have eggs, milk, fresh garlic or a tomato. During our once-yearly shopping trip we learned to buy ingredients in bulk, and ones that could be used for many purposes. Often we found ourselves making unique substitutions, say mayonnaise for sour cream or eggs. All of the vegetables were either canned or reconstituted and sometimes our caribou enchiladas were flavored with spaghetti sauce, extra chili powder and a can of jalapeño peppers.

While in Alaska, we never had more than three kinds of vegetable oil in the house, so take note that almost any of the oils referenced within these pages can be substituted for your oil of choice be it vegetable, canola, olive, grapeseed or peanut. One caution, however, is not to use olive oil for deep or heavy frying as it has a low smoke point, and loses many of its health benefits when heated to high temperatures. Also, substitute what you need to for personal health reasons or to meet special dietary needs. In Indonesia, where we lived after our time in Alaska, everything is cooked and fried using palm oil, which makes for a delicious meal but some very high cholesterol readings. Limit salt, substitute artificial sweeteners and use heatable margarine substitutes for butter when necessary. Bacon, for example, can be parboiled prior to use to cut down on the fat content.

When it comes to flavor preferences in this book, or any recipe for that matter, don't be afraid to implement changes. If a recipe calls for cinnamon and you don't like that spice, simply omit it. For best results try the recipe exactly as written and then take notes on how to change it next time. It's likely you may find many ways to improve upon our recipes in order to meet personal desires.

Easy substitutions can also simplify the cooking process, whereby further saving time and money. Many professionals, for example, balk at the idea of using garlic from a jar, dehydrated onions or diced tomatoes from a can. Obviously, the home cook is sacrificing some flavor for time, but if you have ever cooked with a baby on one shoulder and a toddler clinging to a knee, you know the value of opening a jar or a can for a recipe. In this book we have tried to use a combination of prepared ingredients with the hopes that a cook with more time on his or her hands will simply substitute fresh ingredients when able. Along those same lines, when the recipe calls for three inches of fresh, minced ginger, there is some great minced and pureed ginger sold in jars, in the produce section of most grocery stores, that can be used instead.

Herbs and spices are another area where substitutions are easy and, perhaps, necessary to meet personal preferences. Dried can almost always be substituted for fresh and in many cases certain herbs may be subbed for one another. There are times of the year, for example, when cilantro flourishes in our herb garden, but when it's unavailable, parsley is easily substituted. If running low on both herbs, try a new herb flavor combination. (See below for tips on freezing herbs.)

Spices that are called for in whole-form can be substituted for ground (just use about half as much) while more exotic spices can be omitted if not on hand. Fruit and vegetable substitutions can be treated the same as herb substitutions. A dish will not be ruined if green bell peppers are used in place of red. Shallots can sometimes be difficult to find, so onions can always be substituted.

■ SEASONAL INGREDIENTS

Many of the common ingredients used in this book are considered seasonal. When the garden turns-out a 10-pound box of onions, or the local produce stand has giant bell peppers on sale, 4 for $1.00, don't pass them up. We freeze several seasonal vegetables. Not only does this save money, but later in the year, time is saved as the chopping and dicing is already done; simply take it from the freezer and start cooking.

A food chopper works well for dicing vegetables, and once they've been diced and frozen in snack-size, sealable plastic bags, simply thaw and sauté or add to soup or stew, frozen. Jalapeño peppers are handled similarly, but first the seeds are removed, then it's sliced or diced and stored in small quantities (use rubber gloves when working with chilies). Tiny chili peppers can be placed into freezer bags, seeds intact, and used in small quantities. Be warned though, one hot chili goes a long way and they don't lose their heat in the freezer. Where it may seem like a lot of work spending a few hours chopping and bagging during the summer, efforts pay off the remainder of the year. Even garlic freezes well minced, chopped or whole.

When it comes to sauce shortcuts, try having plenty of tomato-based sauces on hand as well as various types of herb pestos which, add a flavor-punch to many meals. In our garden it seems tomatoes wait till the last minute, then ripen all at once. After a few batches of salsa it's time for something a little easier. Roasted tomatoes in many flavors are a staple to much of our year-round cooking.

■ ROASTED TOMATOES

1. Season tomatoes with different flavor components, such as plain salt and pepper, Italian (red wine, oregano, thyme, garlic, basil), Mexican (cilantro, cumin, garlic, chilies, oregano), Asian (ginger, sesame oil, soy sauce, garlic, lemon or lime), Mediterranean

(rosemary, mint, oregano, parsley). Onions can be added to all of the above flavors. Tuck garlic and herbs up under the whole tomatoes to prevent them from over-browning. More herbs can also be added after cooking to give a more intense flavor.

2. Liberally drizzle olive oil on tomatoes.

3. Roast tomatoes in the oven at 300° 3-5 hours. Tomato flavor becomes more intense the longer the tomatoes cook down and condense.

4. Place tomatoes, juice and all the ingredients in a blender and puree.

5. Pour mixture into freezer containers, label and freeze. Sauce for pasta, soup and stew bases or casserole ingredients are ready, simply unthaw.

Pestos are another family favorite and several of those recipes are listed throughout the book. Either frozen in snack-size, sealable bags or frozen in ice-cube trays and later popped out and put in large sealable bags, there are unlimited uses for these freshly frozen flavor combinations. If a recipe calls for fresh basil or cilantro and there's none on hand, simply unthaw a cube or two of pesto and add as needed.

With the seemingly ever-increasing diversity of pastas, rice and whole grains, there is now more to a meal than *"meat and potatoes."* Most recipes in these pages suggest a side or "serve with" idea, but this is an area in which to exercise creativity as well. To include some fiber, try whole-grain pastas or brown rice. For those with wheat allergies, there are some great rice and/or spelt-based pastas. And for the finicky eater, a trick that has worked with our boys for years is the idea that anything brown has a chocolate base, so whole-wheat pastas are known as *"chocolate pasta"* at our house. What works in one home may not work in another.

■ FREEZING COOKED MEATS

The first few times an entire television production crew showed up for dinner, Tiffany found herself in the kitchen all day. Since then she's learned some tricks to quick preparation for last-minute meals. When pressure cooking, roasting or slow cooking, prepare more than will likely be consumed. Instead of waiting a few days and freezing what you know will not get eaten, immediately portion out food to freeze for later use.

Tex-Mex Filling and Versatile Venison Filling are both recipes in this book designed for the purpose of freezing. Enchiladas, burritos, pasta dishes, beans, stir-frys, pot pies, casseroles and soups can all be prepared quickly with the use of precooked and seasoned meat. Always be sure that there is plenty of liquid in the dish to make up for any moisture lost in the freezing process. Condensed soups and broths can be added to help in this matter.

Due to our limited food options when living in Alaska, we enjoyed many casserole combinations. Nearly anything can become a *"casserole."* The general rule of thumb is to add 1 part meat to 1 part vegetable to 2 parts starch (pasta, rice, potato) a can or two of something creamy, a bit more liquid, some cheese and cover with potato chips, corn flakes or buttered bread crumbs. Bake at 350° for 30-45 minutes, or turn down the heat and keep warm until the hunters get home.

■ FREEZING STOCK

One other item our freezer is filled with is stock or broth. Never does a turkey or chicken carcass go unused in the kitchen. Bones and the bit of meat stuck to them are used to flavor another dish. Be it wild or domesticated meat, homemade stock adds a wonderful richness to many recipes. By simply adding a few onions, some celery and carrots and low boiling on the stove for several hours, what was headed for the garbage becomes something valuable. Once stock has simmered, salt and pepper to taste or add other seasonings if desired. Cool completely and pour into plastic freezer containers. Be sure to label and date stock. Use within three to six months. Stock can be thawed in the refrigerator or microwave prior to use.

■ OTHER SHORTCUTS

Many shortcuts will not produce certain flavor-layering components, but they are still better alternatives to processed foods, frozen dinners and fast-food drive-thrus. Several recipes have suggested shortcuts we've found useful, but don't hesitate to experiment. Often you can prepare a fast-food meal in the slow cooker.

If you like experimenting with new and exotic flavors, simply buy ready-made spice combinations or sauces in a jar and add to your meat, then see what happens. We have discovered many family favorites in this way,

and even though we have found some things we were not fond of, usually we're able to reseason or add to a casserole to save dinner.

Look in your refrigerator and think about what needs to be used up, perhaps a jar of orange marmalade or apricot preserves. Both make great basting sauces, just add a bit of oil and a splash or two or soy or Worcestershire sauce. Capers or green olives added to dishes are great for more zing.

When traveling, try to pick up area-specialties like guava jelly, tropical fruit preserves or specialty chili pastes, again just for the purpose of adding a spoonful to a dish to give it a new flavor element. Always find out if there is a web site or distribution contact, for if

you find something really special it may become a signature dish you will want to repeat over and over again. Keep on hand, packaged gravy and spice mixes in case you run low on fresh ingredients or are in a rush and just want to add water to make gravy instead of whipping it up from scratch. There are also limitless commercial marinades in both liquid and powder form that complement wild game very well.

Whatever it is you're cooking, don't be afraid to substitute flavors to fit your tastes. Experimenting with various ingredients can open up a whole new world, one that, even today, leads many people to discover the pleasures of wild-game.

Recipe Notes

Recipes

VENISON

Index

Cooking Method Index

Oven

Crock Pot Cooking

Grilling

Planking

NOTE: Plank recipes can be used on the grill or in the oven.

Pressure Cooking

Smoking

Stir-Fry

Stove Top

ABOUT THE AUTHORS

ABOUT THE AUTHORS

Scott & Tiffany Haugen were born and raised in Oregon's Willamette Valley, near the breath-taking McKenzie River. Growing up, both families depended on wild game as a staple.

After marriage, Scott & Tiffany spent several years living in the Alaskan Arctic, where they adopted a subsistence lifestyle. Traveling the globe, the couple later called Sumatra, Indonesia home. Together the Haugens have traveled to nearly 30 countries. Today the Haugens live near where they both grew up, raising two sons, Braxton and Kazden.

PLANK COOKING
The Essence of Natural Wood
By Scott & Tiffany Haugen

IN *Plank Cooking: The Essence of Natural Wood,* globe-trotting authors, Scott & Tiffany Haugen, share some of the world's most exquisite flavors. Thai red curry prawns, Achiote pork roast, pesto couscous stuffed chicken, and caramelized bananas are just a few of the unique recipes brought to life in this fully illustrated, one-of-a-kind book.

In the oven or on a grill, plank cooking is fun and simple. This book outlines how to master the art of plank cooking, from seasoning planks to detailed cooking tips in over 100 easy-to-follow recipes. Though exotic tastes prevail, the ingredients used in Plank Cooking are easy to find in most grocery stores. Full color; 6 x 9; 152 pages

Spiral SB: $19.95   **ISBN: 1-57188-332-0**

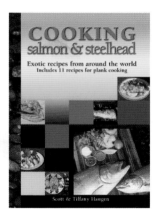

COOKING SALMON & STEELHEAD
Exotic Recipes From Around the World
By Scott & Tiffany Haugen

This is not your grandmother's salmon cookbook. The long-time favorites are included and also unique yet easy-to-prepare dishes, like Cabo fish tacos and Tuscan pesto. This cookbook includes: Appetizers, soups & salads, entrees, one-dish meals, exotic tastes, marinades & rubs, outdoor cooking, pastas, stuffed fish, plank cooking, wine selection, scaling and fileting your catch, choosing market fish, cooking tips, and so much more. The Haugens have traveled to and studied cuisines in countries around the world—including the Caribbean, Asia, and Europe—your kitchen is not complete without a copy of *Cooking Salmon & Steelhead.*

Spiral SB: $24.95   ISBN: 1-57188-291-X

EGG CURES
Proven Recipes & Techniques
By Scott Haugen

Of all the natural baits, many consider eggs to be the best. Before this book, you'd have an easier time getting the secret recipe for Coca-Cola than getting a fisherman to part with his personal egg cure. But now, Scott Haugen has done it for you, he went to the experts—fishermen and fishing guides—to get their favorite egg cures and fishing techniques, plus their secret tricks and tips. The result is this book. These 28 recipes come from anglers who catch fish—read this book and you will too. Guaranteed! 5 1/2 x 8 1/2 inches, 90 pages.

Spiral SB: $15.00   **ISBN: 1-57188-238-3**

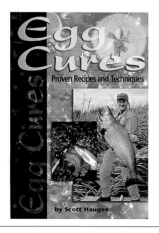

SMOKING SALMON & STEELHEAD

by Scott & Tiffany Haugen

Among the many benefits of fishing is the chance to bring home the occasional salmon for the smoker. But are you tired of using the same old recipe? If so, the Haugens have done all the experimenting for you. The result is this book, filled with 54 wet and dry brine recipes, including: sweet teriyaki, tropical tang, extra hot habenero, sweet & simple, chardonnay splash, spicy sweet, triple pepper, and many, many more. They also share great tips on different smoking woods to use, preparation prior to smoking your fish, cannon smoked salmon, their favorite recipes using smoked salmon, and a section on troubleshooting meant to answer basic questions. If you like smoked salmon, you need this book. 6 x 9 inches, 96 pages, all-color.

Spiral SB: $19.95   **ISBN: 1-57188-290-1**

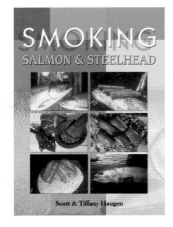

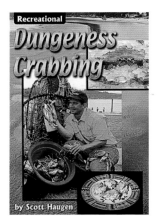

RECREATIONAL DUNGENESS CRABBING

By Scott Haugen

From Alaska to Mexico, Dungeness crabs are pursued for sport and their fine eating quality; *Recreational Dungeness Crabbing* gives you all the information you need to enjoy safe, fun, and productive crabbing. With an emphasis on family, safety, and fun, Haugen covers: natural history of the Dungeness crab; gear; bait; crabbing from a dock or boat; offshore crabbing; raking and dip netting; rod & reel; diving for crabs; crabbing in Oregon and Washington, including hot spots; cleaning and preparing your catch; favorite crab recipes; and more. 6 x 9 inches, 72 pages, full-color.

SB: $12.95   **ISBN: 1-57188-288-X**

SUMMER STEELHEAD
Fishing Techniques

By Scott Haugen

Scott Haugen is quickly becoming known for his fact-filled, full-color fishing books. This time Haugen explores summer steelhead, including: understanding summer steelhead; reading water; bank, drift, and sight fishing; jigs, plugs, lures, dragging flies, and bait; fishing high, turbid waters; tying your own leaders; egg cures; gathering bait; do-it-yourself sinkers; hatchery and recycling programs; mounting your catch; cleaning and preparation; smoking your catch; and more. 6 x 9 inches, 135 pages.

SB: $15.95   **ISBN: 1-57188-295-2**